Noa's Ark

One Child's Voyage into Multiliteracy

David Schwarzer

HEINEMANN
Portsmouth, NH

Heinemann
A division of Reed Elsevier Inc.
361 Hanover Street
Portsmouth, NH 03801–3912
www.heinemann.com

Offices and agents throughout the world

© 2001 by David Schwarzer

The author and publisher wish to thank those who have generously
given permission to reprint borrowed material:

Figure 3–1 is reprinted by permission of School Zone Publishing
Company, Grand Haven, MI. *www.schoolzone.com*

Library of Congress Cataloging-in-Publication Data
Schwarzer, David.
    Noa's ark : one child's voyage into multiliteracy / David Schwarzer.
        p. cm.
    Includes bibliographical references.
    ISBN 0-325-00279-7
    1. Multilingualism in children—United States—Case studies.
    2. Literacy—United States—Case studies.   3. Second language
    acquisition—Case studies.   4. Education, Bilingual—United States—
    Case studies.   I. Title.
    P115.2 .S38 2001
    404'.2'0973—dc21   00-011338

Editor: Lois Bridges
Production: Denise Botelho, Colophon
Production coordinator: Elizabeth Valway
Cover design: Cathy Hawkes, Cat and Mouse
Manufacturing: Louise Richardson

Printed in the United States of America on acid-free paper
05   04   03   02   01   DA   1   2   3   4   5

I would like to dedicate this book to the loving memory of my father, Hirsh León Schwarzer. Special thanks to my loving wife, Taly for her support during this project, and my daughter Noa, for her willingness to let me investigate her multiliteracy development. Many thanks to my mother and my siblings, as well as my father and mother-in-law. I would also like to thank Drs. Ken and Yetta Goodman who have helped me throughout this whole process, becoming dear colleagues and friends; Dr. Dana Fox for her input and help with my English writing; and Dr. Terry Green, a dear friend and colleague.

אני מקדיש ספר זה לאישתי האהובה, טלי, אשר תמכה בי לאורך כל הדרך:
במעבר לארץ אחרת, בתמיכה הנפשית והכלכלית במשך שלוש השנים של
הפרויקט. תודה מיוחדת לבתי נעה, אשר אפשרה לי להביט מקרוב על
התפתחות האוריינית שלה. אני רוצה להודות למשפחתי, אישתי, משפחת קזז על
עזרתם הרבה ובמיוחד לסבא רפי ולסבתא רבקה. תודה מיוחדת לסבתא הכי
טובה בעולם, סבתא מלכה בקר.

Quisiera dedicar este libro a la memoria de mi querido padre Hirsh León Schwarzer, que seguramente estaría muy orgulloso de mi trabajo, y a mi familia: especialmente a mi madre, Cecilia Kasirer de Schwarzer, por su ayuda y apoyo durante todo este largo proceso; y a mis hermanos: José y Sara. Quisiera también agradecer a mi estudiante Mary Petrón por su ayuda

Contents

Contents

Introduction

A Multiliteracy Journey Begins

The book you are about to read is the final step of a one-year research journey studying my seven-year-old daughter Noa's writing development in English, Hebrew, and Spanish. The primary foci of this book are to document and analyze how a particular child develops literacy in three languages, both in the home and at school, and to help monolingual mainstream teachers foster second-language learners' development of literacy in English as well as in their first languages.

During the past few years, the number of second-language learners has increased dramatically in most public school districts in the United States. At the same time, most monolingual mainstream classroom teachers lack English as a Second Language (ESL) training. According to the office of Bilingual education and Minority Language Affairs, more than 25 percent of the school teachers reported to have ESL students in their classrooms, but 70 percent of these teachers said they received no ESL academic preparation. Moreover, most teachers in the United States seem to be very concerned about helping students develop English literacy as soon as possible. Teachers seem to view biliteracy development (the development of literacy in two languages) or multiliteracy development (the development of literacy in more than two languages) as something difficult or even unattainable. The scope of this book is to both allow the reader to follow closely one child's multiliteracy development (including successful experiences and less successful experiences) as well as create a deeper understanding of common practices used by Noa's teachers that may serve to foster or inhibit multiliteracy development.

During this case study, I followed Noa's early multiliteracy development in the community in which she lived, in her household, and at her school. She experienced the use of three languages in her trilingual family and with people with whom she interacted linguistically.

My main research goal is to show the complexity of the multiliteracy development of a first grader in the context of her daily life, in which three languages are present in different formats, for different purposes and audiences. My main practical goal is to show how the role of the teacher is pivotal in order to develop early multiliteracy development.

Noa's context for literacy development may seem unusual in the United States, where a single language is dominant. However, in many parts of the world, it's not unusual for students of her age to be immersed in multilingual and multiliterate environments.

While writing these pages, I always have in mind the interests of bilingual and biliterate children by showing that the development of multiliteracy isn't impossible or unattainable, but, on the contrary, can be developed easily in schools, depending on the context of its development and the functional need to be literate in more than one language. On the other hand, I also have in mind how this book can serve monolingual teachers in the development of some strategies and tools that may help them foster multiliteracy development in their early childhood classrooms.

Seizing New Territory

The term *early multiliteracy development* deserves some explanation. Kelder (1996) asserts that there is a need to define and recognize nonschooled literacies associated with different tools and mediums as well as literacies associated with using information and technology. He states that "*multilit eracies* must be studied in many contexts to better understand their role in instruction and curriculum development." According to this definition, there are different literacies (visual literacy, mathematical literacy, music literacy, computer literacy, and so on). Schools should construct a multiliterate curriculum in order to foster all of these different literacies in the school setting.

In this book I define the term *early multiliteracy development* differently. For many years, oral language development researchers have written about "language development," "bilingualism," and "multilingualism." Using this same English pattern, other researchers are writing about "literacy development" and "biliteracy development." In this book, I introduce the use of the term *early multiliteracy development* simply as the development of early multiple written languages simultaneously.

To Be or Not to Be Multiliterate, That's the Question!

For many years, there has been a "debate" surrounding bilingualism in early childhood. McLaughlin (1984) states three different basic positions about early bilingualism: the maximalist position, the minimalist position, and the intermediate position:

> Those who take a maximalist position hold that early bilingualism is essentially a positive experience for children. . . . The minimalist position holds that early bilingualism has little—or even a negative—effect on children. . . . There is an intermediate position possible between the extreme maximalist and the minimalist ones. (43–44)

Today, there is still a lot of controversy about this debate. This book is based on the assumption that early bilingualism is essentially a positive experience when it is pursued under the "right" conditions, such as community involvement, cultural understanding, and functional application in the school and home settings. This book is based on an in-depth case study employing ethnographic and linguistic techniques to document the development of a multilingual first grader in her home and school environments. Numerous studies done in multilingual and multiliterate immigrant settings attempted to analyze the knowledge created and used in the home environment and its implications in the classroom. Delgado-Gaitan and Trueba (1991) studied a group of Mexican-American families, having in mind their participation in their own community. These authors were interested in the literacy practices at home and in the school. In their research, they viewed the home setting and the school setting as a dichotomy: In the home, the children use and learn languages in context, while at school they are asked only to learn language in isolation and out of context. In my work, I use the idea of "funds of knowledge" (Moll 1988) as a more comprehensive way to see the interactions between school activities and home activities and their implications for multiliteracy. According to Moll, both schools and house use languages in different ways. Schools and house do teach language, sometimes in context and sometimes in isolation. Most middle class children bring to the school funds of knowledge that are valued and useful in the school curriculum. On the other hand, minority language students do have funds of knowledge that are developed in their communities, but are seldom valued in the school setting. In this book, I am looking for the situations in which the funds of knowledge of Noa were utilized in the school and how they impacted her multiliteracy development. Moreover, children's home languages are funds of knowledge for these children.

The main purpose of this book then, is to explore early multiliteracy development in a personal and social perspective. Therefore, research from different areas, such as early literacy development, biliteracy development, and multicultural education, will be presented.

The first part of this book, Chapters 1 through 4, is based on Goodman and Wilde's (1992) description of the three different interactive aspects of the writing process: the literacy community, the writer, and the written text. I used their categories to organize the social context and linguistic history of Noa. In Chapter 1, I present the writer and the literacy communities in which she lives. In order to do so, I describe in detail the multilingual background of Noa's family as well as her literacy communities. Chapters 2 through 4 deal with the properties of the texts Noa constructed throughout the study. In Chapter 2, I analyze Noa's written texts in terms of their forms and functions. In Chapter 3, I analyze Noa's literacy development in general, according to three different tensions: convention versus invention, home versus school, and student-centered versus teacher-centered editing. In Chapter 4, I analyze Noa's multiliteracy development in particular.

The second part of this book deals with practical strategies and tools that could be used by monolingual mainstream teachers in order to foster early multiliteracy development in their classes. Chapter 5 lists a series of practical ideas and tools developed as a result of the research study and of presentations of this research across the world.

1

The Literacy Community and the Writer: Noa's Sociolinguistic Contexts for Multiliteracy Development

How Do You Learn French? You Travel to France!

We are in the family room. Noa is watching TV, and there is an advertisement about using audiocassettes once a day for one hour in order to learn how to speak French.

Noa: They don't know anything!

David: What do you mean?

Noa: That's not the way to learn a new language!!

David: How do you learn a new language?

Noa: You need to go to a place that people speak that language. At the beginning, you don't understand anything, but little by little you understand everything.

David: Mmm . . .

Noa: Do you remember me? I did not know a word in English when we came to Tucson, but now I can understand everything.

(This conversation was translated from Hebrew to English)

Noa knows from her own personal experience that the use of any audiocassette once a day is not going to be enough to develop a new language. She remembers very vividly her first days in Tucson. While studying Noa, I asked her if we could have prepared her in any way for her stay in the United States. She replied,

> I don't think so. You need to hear the language for a while. Then, you need to try to speak it. If the people understand what you said, you keep doing it. If they don't, you find another way to say it.

Noa's story illustrates what teachers have known for many years: Young children develop their knowledge about literacy in the social context of their lives in their family, school, and community. Writing develops differently, depending on the particular sociolinguistic context in which it occurs. Goodman and Wilde (1992) described three different interactive aspects of the writing process: the literacy community, the writer, and the written text. I used these categories to organize the social context and linguistic history of Noa. First, let me introduce Noa, the writer.[1]

Description of the Writer

Noa was born in Israel on January 16, 1988. During her first year, I spoke to Noa only in Spanish. Taly (Noa's mom) spoke to her only in Hebrew. We hired a Spanish-speaking

---

[1]While you read this detailed account of Noa's background, have in mind that the purpose of this information is to show teachers the importance of students' language backgrounds. We should create ways to know our students particular background related to language usage. We may use questionnaires for this purpose, we may compose a family language usage tree (explained later), or we may just ask these questions during our first interview with our students.

woman to stay with Noa while we were at work. She spoke to Noa in Spanish. As a baby, Noa responded both to Hebrew and to Spanish. However, Noa's first words were in Hebrew. Because of the wonder of hearing my daughter speak Hebrew, I did not maintain the use of Spanish when she started speaking in Hebrew; therefore, Noa does understand Spanish, but she does not speak it.

In Israel, my wife and I were professional teachers. After I finished my M.A. in education from the Tel-Aviv University, we decided to go to the United States so I could study for my Ph.D. It is common practice among scholars in Israel to go abroad for advanced graduate studies. Many go to Europe and others go to the United States.

When we came to the United States in July of 1992, Noa (age 4.6) did not know any English. For example, when we went to the pool in the apartment complex where we lived, she wasn't able to communicate with the children, she was unable to understand TV or to answer the telephone.

Between August of 1992 and Chanukah (December of 1992), she became proficient in English, sounding like an American. She was able to participate in conversations and answer the questions of English speakers, play and converse with English-speaking children, and enjoy English TV. This is not unusual, because Noa was one of the only students at her private preschool that spoke Hebrew. She was faced with one of the most common experiences facing English as a Second Language (ESL) students in this country: the sink-or-swim option. Noa was lucky! She learned how to swim pretty fast!

When Noa was ready to go to first grade, we made a decision to send her to a public school. We became interested in the bilingual Spanish/English first grade in the school. We asked the principal to place her in the bilingual class. The principal explained that she did not need to go to the bilingual program because "she speaks English very well." Noa was placed in the monolingual first grade class. After two weeks of classes in the monolingual English class, and only after a long conversation with the principal of the school, Noa was transferred to the first grade bilingual Spanish/English class.

Languages and the Contexts of Their Use in Noa's Language Development

Clearly, Noa is immersed in an environment in which Hebrew, Spanish, and English are present in the different contexts (home, school, and community) of her life. I think that this description is extremely important in order to really understand the way that Noa perceives literacy development in general and multiliteracy development in particular. Following is a detailed description of the contexts of the uses of each language and the ways the three languages intermingle and come into contact with each other.

Hebrew

Hebrew is present orally on a daily basis, because it's the main language of communication at home. Taly, Noa's mother, and I try to speak to each other and to Noa in Hebrew as much as possible. Many times Noa speaks to us in English, especially if the theme of the talk is related to an experience that occurred in the United States, but we try to answer in Hebrew.

Taly and I are Hebrew teachers in the United States. Therefore, books, report cards, materials, exams, and other written materials in Hebrew are visible and available all the time. We receive a weekly newspaper in Hebrew, and we write on a bilingual Hebrew/English computer, so Noa sees us reading and writing Hebrew. In her two years at a Jewish preschool, Hebrew was present orally in prayers every day and in songs on Fridays. In the school setting, written Hebrew was present only as letters that were painted or traced. Once a week, the new letter of the week was introduced, following the alphabetic order. The children learned the name of the letter of the week and traced it into a notebook. Neither children nor teachers in the preschool wrote or read in Hebrew. Some Hebrew letters were used as ornaments in the classes, and sometimes the teacher used work sheets of some Hebrew letters for the children to color. When we came to the United States, we brought approximately one hundred children's books in Hebrew to read to and with Noa. These books included fiction, nonfiction, dictionaries, folk tales, and so forth. Taly and I read to Noa at least three times a week, usually in Hebrew. We participate with the Israeli community in informal gatherings of children and adults, and the spoken language among the adults is Hebrew. However, the children use English in their play, but they speak Hebrew when they're interacting with an adult.

Spanish

Spanish is present in all the communication with the family members on Noa's paternal side. For example, when my mother comes to visit us from Israel, or when I speak with my brother or sister on the phone, we use Spanish. Some of my friends in Tucson are Spanish speakers; therefore, there are instances in which Noa listens to our Spanish conversations. Because Noa is in a bilingual Spanish/English first grade class at school, Spanish is available to her every day of the week. In our house, we do not own many books in Spanish, but I borrow some from school. Occasionally (once a month), I read Noa a children's book in Spanish, mostly related to the themes and words learned at school. The times when I ty to read a children's book in Spanish, Noa resists the experience, telling me that she does not know any Spanish.

Taly and I do not use written Spanish as much as we use written English and Hebrew, but some of the professional books and articles that I read and write are in Spanish.

English

English is present in our home every day through the TV, the daily newspaper, the report cards and announcements for the school, and so on. I write all of my university papers in English. English is the predominant written and spoken language in Noa's life in the United States. Although Taly and I prefer to read to Noa in Hebrew or Spanish, Noa has a lot of books in English that she likes to read by herself and asks other English speakers to read to her. These include children's dictionaries, fiction, and nonfiction books; calendars; games; and so forth. At the present time, on average, we read to her two times a week in Hebrew, once a week in English, and once a month in Spanish.

Multilingualism and Code Switching

In the area of bilingualism and multilingualism, there are different philosophical positions regarding the best way to immerse children in bilingual and multilingual environments. Leopold (1939), in his ground-breaking research about his child's bilingualism, avoided mixing the two languages that he was trying to investigate: He spoke to the child in one language, while his wife spoke to the child in the other language. Leopold was creating an environment that was different from the environment in which most bilingual families find themselves, where languages are mixed.

In our case, Noa has been a social participant in many literacy events in which code switching between languages takes place. Code switching is the alternation between languages, within or between utterances (Poplack 1983). In our family, languages are spoken, taking into consideration the context of the oral/written event, the audience, the topic, the participants in the conversation, the willingness or unwillingness of the participants to be understood, and the traditions (especially in ritualistic practices).

Sometimes, Noa listens to Taly and I code switching to Spanish when we do not want her to understand. Other times, she hears us saying to her that now that she understands a little bit more Spanish, we need to find a new language to use between us. On other occasions, Spanish is present when I speak with my family on the phone or when they visit me; and we use Hebrew with our Israeli friends in the United States, as well as English in my work and my writings.

Code switching in writing as well as in speaking is frequent in our household, and it is used sometimes as a stylistic device. Code-switched words, expressions, or even sentences can give the reader or the listener a "taste" of the experience. Some writers that use different written languages to communicate to each other code switch between them as a stylistic device; for example, "Le compré a Amit un aftershave" ("I bought Amit a bottle of aftershave lotion") When my sister wrote this sentence in her letter, she could have used Spanish for the word *aftershave (colonia para después de afeitarse)*. Instead, she used the English code-switched word *aftershave*. Her use of a code-switched word did not imply her lack of knowledge of the Spanish word, but the preference of using the term in English in order to write not only the facts of the event, but also the "taste" of it.

Mixing languages or maintaining a separation between them is often a main concern of researchers and teachers in the area of bilingual education. Many researchers of bilingual education are coming to accept code switching as "an effective teaching and learning strategy" (Quintero & Huerta 1990). Research shows bilingual grammatical competence on the part of speakers who code switched between languages (Huerta 1977; Pfaff 1979; Poplack 1983). Code switching also can enhance communication and learning in bilingual communities (Aguirre 1988; Tukinoff 1985).

In a few words, Noa was immersed not only in a linguistic situation in which three languages were present, but also in a situation in which the languages were used in a code-switched mode in oral language as well as in written language.

Description of Noa's Multiliteracy Communities

As Goodman and Wilde (1992) states,

> Communities of students in schools cannot be separated from the communities of their homes, villages, towns and cities. The social history children bring to school represents the language, beliefs, and knowledge of their community, and affects both their writing and their view of themselves as writers. We can observe the similarities among all young writers and at the same time come to understand the unique individual and social differences among children and the communities in which they live. (xiv)

Therefore, it is appropriate to describe the family and community linguistic experiences and histories that influence Noa's multilingual literacy development.

Noa's Family
I decided to do a language family tree of Noa's family to show the written, read, and spoken histories that became the multilingual environment of Noa's development. I traced

the multilingual nature of Noa's family back three generations, from her parents to her grandparents and great-grand-
parents.

It's necessary to provide this linguistic, nationality, and
ethnic information regarding Noa's family and communities
in order to see its effect in her multiliteracy development. I
believe, as Schieffelin and Cochran-Smith (1984) do, that the
development of multiliteracy docs not emerge "naturally,"
but as a result of the actions, beliefs, and attitudes of the
learner's community:

> The point that we want to stress is that the children's in-
> terest on print in this community (or in any community)
> does not emerge "naturally" at all. Rather, in this commu-
> nity they emerge out of a particular cultural orientation in
> which literacy is assumed and which organizes children's
> early print experiences in particular ways. (p. 6)

As stated by Schieffelin and Cochran-Smith, Noa has
had a very particular set of experiences since she was born.
Noa's family could be considered eccentric and atypical in a
country like the United States, in which monolingual, mono-
cultural families seem to be the norm. On the other hand,
many families in Israel share similar backgrounds and experiences with Noa. I believe there are similar linguistic histories among families in the United States as well. Figure 1–1
provides an overview of each generation of Noa's an-
tecedents, the languages they use, and whether they use
them in speaking (S), reading (R), or writing (W). A key at
the bottom of the illustration explains the codes used. The
figure is explained further by a narrative discussion.

While reading this detailed description, have in mind
that Noa's teacher was completely unaware of Noa's Language Family Tree. I am arguing that, as teachers, we
should ask our students about their literacy experiences at
home and in their communities. In many cases, we may

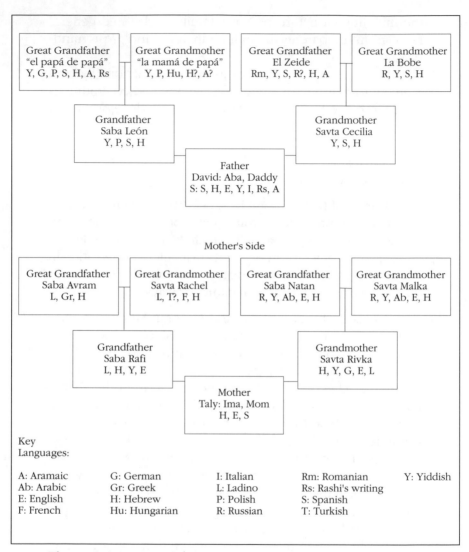

Figure 1–1 Noa's Family Language Use Tree

find multilingual households and language communities in our schools. Some kind of language family tree may be used as a first tool in order to map students' languages.

Noa's Family Literacy History from Her Father's Side I describe Noa's family in terms of languages usage (see Figure 1–1). In describing Noa's family, I paid attention for the first time to the names of the participants in this story. The names of the members of the family (see top of Figure 1–1) are in four different languages, and sometimes they are code-switched forms: El Zeide is what we all called Noa's great-grandfather from my mother's side. The form used for his name is a code-switched form using the male singular Spanish article ("el") and the Yiddish word for grandfather ("Zeide"). I decided to call the participants by their name in our family, because even naming practices reveal how multilingualism is embedded in the everyday language in Noa's life.

"El papá de papá" (Noa's great-grandfather on my father's side) was born in Austria. He fought for the Austrian government in World War I. When he was young, he emigrated to Poland, and in 1932, he immigrated again to Argentina. "El papá de papá" held the highly respected profession (within the Jewish community) of copying sacred texts like Bibles and prayer books. He was a "Sofer Stam" in Poland. In Argentina, he became a merchant. He did not want his family to come to Argentina because he was afraid they would lose their Jewish identity. He knew how to read and write in Rashi's writing. (Rashi is a Jewish exegete to the Bible who invented a different Hebrew writing system used only in his interpretations of the Bible. All of his explanations are written in his special way and are called Rashi's writing.)

According to family stories, "el papá de papá" corresponded with his wife and family for seven years from Argentina, sending letters in Yiddish. In Argentina, he learned to speak and read Spanish, but he did not do much writing in the Spanish language. In Argentina, he read a newspaper written in Yiddish, Di Presse, as well as one written in Polish.

"La mamá de papá" was born in Hungary during the Austrian–Hungarian empire. She immigrated to Poland when she was young, and in 1939, she immigrated with her children to Argentina, where her husband was waiting for her.

Noa's grandfather, Saba León (Grandpa León), the first son of "el papá de papá" and "la mamá de papá," was born in Poland. His family was very poor, and they endured many attacks against the Jewish people. In 1939, at age 13, Saba León immigrated with "la mamá de papá" and his brothers to Argentina. When he came to Argentina, he preferred to speak and read in Polish rather than in Yiddish. However, after some years, he forgot his Polish, and he wasn't able to speak or read it any more. Saba León never became an Argentinean citizen, and in many ways he never felt like one. He learned Spanish while working for the economic survival of his family. However, he had regular instruction in Spanish at a public night school for immigrants. He wrote many letters in Spanish to my brother and myself after we immigrated to Israel. Saba León knew how to read the Hebrew prayers by memory, but he did not understand what he was reading.

"El Zeide," Noa's great-grandfather from my mother's side, was born in Romania. At the age of 17, in order to avoid being drafted for service by the Romanian army, he immigrated to Argentina by himself. (His family that remained in Romania immigrated to Israel after the Holocaust, and they live today in Beer Sheva, Israel). El Zeide knew how to speak, read, and write in Yiddish. He knew how to read in Hebrew and Aramaic for the basic Jewish prayers. He knew how to speak, read, and write in basic communicational Spanish. He also spoke some Russian with his wife when he did not want the children to understand.

"La Bobe" (a code-switched form using the Spanish female article, "la" and the Yiddish word for grandma, "bobe") was born in Besarabia, a part of today's Moldavia in Russia. La Bobe was known in the family for her criticism of the schooling system in Besarabia. She learned how to read and write in the Russian education system, but at home she mainly spoke Yiddish. She knew how to read and write in Yiddish. She learned how to speak Spanish, but I remember her speaking to me mostly in Yiddish. I do not remember seeing her reading Hebrew from a prayer book. She knew some basic religious prayers by heart, but I do not think that she could read in Hebrew or Aramaic.

Noa's grandmother's (Savta Cecilia [Grandma Cecilia]) first language was Yiddish. However, like most first-generation Argentineans, she did not learn how to read or write in Yiddish, and, for the most part, she refused to speak it. Argentina is a country of immigrants. Most of the first-generation parents wanted their children to learn how to speak their native language (in this case Yiddish). However, the "melting pot" metaphor is part of the mainstream educational system in Argentina. Today, Savta Cecilia can understand almost everything in Yiddish, but she can speak it for only very basic conversation. In 1983, she immigrated to Israel with her family. As new immigrants, the family was offered a six-month program, an "Ulpan," which is a special immersion language program for new immigrants to learn how to read, write, and speak Hebrew. Savta Cecilia always says how hard it was for them, as adults, to learn a new language and to adjust to a new culture.

After Saba León's death, Savta Cecilia developed a relationship with Shlomo, a gentleman friend who was born in Turkey. He speaks mostly Hebrew with her, but in family gatherings he speaks Ladino (an ancient version of Spanish with Hebrew borrowings, spoken in the Jewish communities that were expelled from Spain in 1492).

"Aba," or "Daddy" (that is Noa's name for me), was born to a family in which many languages were present. I was also introduced to other languages through instruction. From kindergarten to high school, I was sent to a private Jewish school in which Spanish was taught in the morning and Hebrew speaking, reading, and writing was taught in the afternoon. In secondary school, I had classes of English (three years), Latin (three years), Italian (two years), and Yiddish (five years).

In August 1982, when I was 17, I immigrated to Israel. Hebrew became the main language of communication outside the family. My brother was already in Israel, and my parents, with my sister, followed in December of 1982. In 1992, Taly, Noa, and I came to the United States so that I could study for my Ph.D. in education. Since then, English has become a very important part of our daily communication outside of the family.

Noa's Family Literacy History from Her Mother's Side Noa's great-grandmother on her maternal side is Savta Malka. She came to Israel from Lithuania as a young teenager in 1929, with Yiddish as her mother tongue. At that time, there was a social and political convention in "Palestine" (before the creation of the state of Israel) not to speak Yiddish, because Yiddish was considered the language of Jews in exile. Therefore, Savta Malka and Saba Natan spoke almost entirely in Hebrew. Today, Savta Malka sometimes speaks in Yiddish to her daughter (Savta Rivka), and Savta Rivka replies in Hebrew. I asked Savta Malka why she speaks in Yiddish now when she did not earlier in her life. She replied that today she isn't afraid that Hebrew will not be the language of the State of Israel, so she can speak whatever language she wants!

Saba Natan, Noa's maternal great-grandfather, was born in Lithuania. In 1929, when he was a teenager, he immigrated to Palestine. He was one of the first in Israel to introduce roof tiles. The Nazi soldiers killed Saba Natan's family during World War II.

Savta Rivka, Noa's maternal grandmother, is a first-generation Israeli. She grew up in the city and in a kibbutz (an Israeli socialist agrarian community). Today she lives in Eilat, a city in the south of Israel, with her husband (Saba Rafi). She can read and write in Hebrew, can speak English, German, and Ladino, and can read and write some English and German.

Noa's great-grandfather on her mother's paternal side, Saba Avram, was born in Greece. In 1933, as a young father of two children, he immigrated to Israel with his family. He worked for the first Jewish bus company in Palestine, Drom Yehuda, that in time became Eged, the national bus company of Israel. He spoke, read, and wrote Ladino (the language of the Jewish people in Greece), Greek, and Hebrew.

Noa's great-grandmother on her mother's paternal side, Savta Rachel, was born in Turkey but immigrated to Greece when she was in her early twenties and married. She was very beautiful and from a very rich family. She studied at the French school, The Alliance Francaise; therefore, she spoke, wrote and read French better than she did Turkish. She also spoke, read, and wrote in Ladino, the language that she used at home.

Noa's maternal grandfather, Saba Rafi, was born in Greece. When he was 5 years old, his family immigrated to Palestine. He was involved in underground experiences of a political nature before Israel become a state. He fought in many battles until he was wounded. He celebrates his birthday on the day that he was wounded and survived. Saba Rafi knows how to read and write in Hebrew and Ladino. He learned how to speak Yiddish from Savta Rivka, and Savta Rivka learned how to speak Ladino from Saba Rafi.

Taly, Noa's mother ("Ima", or "Mom"), is a second-generation Israeli. She was born in Tel-Aviv, and when she was 8 years old, the whole family moved to Eilat because of the climate. (Taly's brother had asthma attacks, and the only solution was to move to a dry climate.) Taly knows how to speak, read, and write in Hebrew and English, and she can speak Spanish. She learned Spanish from participating in oral conversations with my family.

Noa likes Savta Malka very much. She is the only great-grandparent that she knows. Although she never met her paternal grandfather and the other grandparents, stories about their lives are told during family gatherings. It's clear from the literature that language stories and the participation in literacy events are a very important part of the individual experiences of children and have a strong influence on their language uses and development. The description of Noa's family language stories is important to show the particular environment in which Noa is growing up.

Noa often asks about Saba León (Grandpa León). In my stories to her, there are several events in which "language stories" are present (Harste et al. 1984). For example, I sing the Polish national anthem because my father sang it to us in Polish. Noa knows that I can understand some Yiddish because that was the first language my father spoke to me when I was a child and I took five years of Yiddish in high school.

In July of 1994 (at the beginning of this research), we traveled as a family to Argentina. My uncles, who usually speak Spanish, spoke in Yiddish to each other, especially when the topic was politics (so those who were not part of the group could not understand). Noa was experiencing a similar linguistic event that I remember experiencing in my childhood.

Another language story that we often retell in the family is about the first meeting between my family (who spoke mostly in Spanish) and Taly (my Hebrew-speaking wife). It was a very difficult moment for everyone: My parents wanted Taly to feel comfortable, so they decided to speak Hebrew. However, their basic vocabulary did not allow them to communicate more than the most basic information. Taly, from her part, wanted us to have a nice time and she wanted us to talk Spanish as we usually did. It was a very tense moment, in which Noa's grandparents realized that they might never be able to fully communicate with their daughter-in-law.

Noa likes to listen to stories about how my siblings and I enjoyed our weekly Sunday trips to La Bobe and El Zeide. We talk about the noise in the house due to all the different languages that were spoken seemingly simultaneously: Yiddish, Spanish, and Russian.

Noa's Language Communities

Noa is very well aware of the transitional situation in which she lives. She knows that we are in the United States for a purpose. She often says that she wants to go home, meaning back to Israel. Her communities of friends in Tucson belong to four different communities: the Jewish community, the Israeli community, the community of Ph.D. candidates from the University of Arizona, and Noa's school community.

The Jewish Community of Tucson Noa went to a Jewish preschool for two years. I was a teacher of Hebrew at the university, and my wife was a teacher of Hebrew in the Hebrew school. We both taught Hebrew once a week for students at the high school level. Our commitment to the Jewish community was very different than the commitment of some of our American Jewish friends. Although we shared the same religious background, we felt like outsiders; we did not belong to the mainstream of the American Jewish community. The Jewish community in Tucson is very formal. In order to become a member, you need to pay an annual fee and participate in events that, in most of the cases, include donations. In this community, Hebrew and English are present all the time. Most of the prayers are recited and chanted in Hebrew. Not much speaking and writing is produced in Hebrew. English is the main language of communication and teaching.

The Israeli Community of Tucson Most of the fifty Israeli families living in Tucson are somehow connected to the University of Arizona. They came to Tucson because one or more members in the family were enrolled as doctoral or postdoctoral students, and most of them will return to Israel at the end of their studies. For this reason, there is no official Israeli community with any kind of building, agenda, or fee. Our Israeli community is made up of individuals who gather together because of mutual needs or interests.

There is another group of Israelis that came as students or as regular residents in order to become permanent residents in Tucson. Both types of Israeli families are part of Noa's social community. We met with this group of friends every weekend, celebrated the Jewish holidays together, and went for trips outside the city. We helped each other find jobs and helped with child care, with religious events, and so on.

The Israeli community members use both English and Hebrew in reading, writing, and speaking. However, Hebrew is the predominant language at home, and English is the predominant language at work.

The Community of Ph.D. Candidates from the University of Arizona The Language, Reading, and Culture (LRC) Department in which I studied was a pleasant surprise. In my previous experience at the University of Tel-Aviv, students worked mostly in isolation. Sometimes they met for a specific project or research, but the program did not provide invitations or opportunities to gather and form a community of learners. In LRC, because one objective of the program is to involve their Ph.D. candidates with the ways of good teaching, many efforts were made to encourage an active community of students. By Labor Day, during our first year, we were invited as a family to Ken and Yetta Goodman's house for the picking of olives with Ken and Yetta's current students. A week after Labor Day, an international potluck was held at the university with the participation of all the professors and graduate students of LRC. Events like these took place in our department on a regular basis, and Noa was present at each of these events. The interactions Noa had with the graduate students interested in the language development of children were very important to her language development. At our next gathering, during Chanukah, Noa was praised by all of the participants for her English. At most of the events, people told Noa that her father spoke about her in class; other students read children's books to her or asked her about her language development.

Noa's School Community Taly and I wanted Noa to start first grade in an American public school. We wanted her to study in a bilingual class in order to expand on the Spanish she was using at home. We also wanted her to have the experience of friends in the neighborhood. Therefore, six months before the school year started, I went to the neighborhood school in order to find out what needed to be done to place Noa in a bilingual class. School personnel told me that there are always some openings for first grade, so I should return during the first few weeks of August.

In August 1994, I went to enroll Noa in the school, and I was told there was no place for her in the bilingual class. I was upset and disappointed. I spoke with the principal, and I tried to explain to him what my understanding had been.

He was surprised that I wanted to send my child to a bilingual class, but he was very supportive. He recommended that I place Noa in a monolingual class for a while. He promised me that in two weeks he would try to have a bilingual placement for her.

Noa started in her monolingual English class, and I made clear to the teacher that we were expecting to have a place for her in the bilingual class. The teacher thought that was a very good idea. She also was very supportive. During this waiting time, I went to the district to see about the possibilities of Noa attending a bilingual class in another school. I thought that, because she was bilingual, the district needed to place her in a bilingual class. They told me that Noa isn't "entitled by law to a bilingual class, since she isn't 'bilingual.'" I was shocked. Noa is bilingual in Hebrew and English, but for the authorities in the district, she wasn't considered bilingual because she wasn't an English and Spanish bilingual.

After two weeks, the principal told us that there was a place for Noa in the bilingual class. Noa wasn't sure if she wanted to move, but after thinking about it, she decided to move to the bilingual class because she also wanted to develop her Spanish.

In the bilingual class, most of the students were from a Spanish-speaking background. Half of them were called Spanish-dominant, and half of them were called English-dominant. During the school day, the class was divided between the Spanish group and the English group. A paraprofessional aide taught the Spanish group, while the teacher taught the English group. In the afternoon, the class worked together on themes such as math, science, art, physical education, and so forth. The teacher usually used both English and Spanish in a translation mode. For example, she gave directions in English, and then she translated the directions into Spanish.

Noa was soon disappointed because she realized she wasn't learning as much Spanish as she wanted. Noa was learning in the English group. Therefore, she did not participate in any of the Spanish group activities. We decided to speak with her teacher. The teacher suggested that Noa could join the Spanish group once a week on Fridays. She predicted that this change would help Noa's development of Spanish literacy.

Noa's class had a lot of books in Spanish and English. The children pledged allegiance to the flag of the United States in English and in Spanish. They sang songs in both languages. However, the teacher and the teacher aide carried on the language instruction as described above.

Noa did not succeed in finding many friends to play with in the afternoon after school. She invited them, but the parents did not allow the children to come and visit.

Noa's class came to our house during Succoth, a Jewish holiday in which a temporary tent is built outside the house. They enjoyed the story and the refreshments. During the year, I went to the class many times, once at Chanukah to light the Chanukah candles; another time, Noa and I read a children's book in Hebrew to the whole class.

Noa's background and language knowledge was used as a resource in her class, and she felt confident enough to tell the children and the teacher stories about Israel and her Jewish heritage.

What We Learned from Noa's Sociocultural Contexts

Issues Related to Family Language Use
Several characteristics of language use emerged as a result of the detailed analysis of Noa's family tree and Noa's

language communities. These major categories are idio-syncratic to Noa's family. However, I will argue that many multilingual and bilingual families use similar strategies while they use different languages in their lives.

Language as an Inclusive Device
Languages change according to the audience. If the audience is multilingual, the language to be used most of the time is chosen according to the language spoken by the majority. For example, I speak Spanish with my brother; then if Taly joins in the conversation, we will shift to Hebrew; but if some English-only-speaking person joins us, we will shift to English, because then everyone can participate. The same pattern of inclusion was used by my family in Argentina, shifting between Yiddish and Spanish, taking into account the language of all the speakers.

Language as an Exclusive Device
Sometimes, the participants in a conversation may purpose-fully communicate in a specific language so the other members of the group will not understand. For example, El Zeide and La Bobe used Russian when they did not want their children to understand; my parents used Yiddish until I started learning and understood it; and Taly and I use Spanish when we do not want Noa to understand. But in the last few months, as Noa seems to understand more and more Spanish, we are not able to use Spanish in such situations. In a monolingual situation, parents sometimes use spelling as a secret code in order to communicate when they do not want their children to understand. In such settings, language is used to exclude others.

Language Learned by Experience
From the description of Noa's background, there are primar-ily two ways through which new or additional languages are learned: by either immigration or marriage. This more fully

explains her comment on the need to go to France in order to learn French.

Immigration Most members of Noa's family and community are immigrants. For example: "el papá de papá"—from Austria to Poland and then to Argentina; Saba León—from Poland to Argentina and then to Israel; Daddy, Aba—from Argentina to Israel and now to the United States. It's clear that the experience of moving to another country involves a change of language and context in which the new language is learned, providing an authentic and natural environment.

Marrying a Spouse Who Speaks Another Language Many of Noa's family and friends learned a new language as a result of a marriage to a person from another country. For example, Saba Rafi learned how to speak Yiddish from Savta Rivka, and Savta Rivka learned how to speak Ladino from Saba Rafi. Taly learned how to speak Spanish through being married to me.

Children Learn the Language of the Country

The children in Noa's community were always the first to more fully develop the new language, and they were a catalyst into the new culture. Family stories reveal that La Bobe learned a lot of things from her children. She was introduced to soap operas in Spanish; while Savta Cecilia learned about Israeli culture through her children. And now Taly and I learn a lot of new customs about the United States and Tucson from Noa.

Language Viewed as a Resource

In all of Noa's language communities and family's experiences, the importance of languages is always clear. Noa's English development was always celebrated. The underlying assumption is that knowledge of a new language can help people survive better in a new country. Saba León used to say that furniture or gold can be taken away from you, but knowledge and a new language can easily be taken from one place to the other, and nobody can take them away from you.

Noa's family history is very distinctive: Her family uses different languages for different purposes; her family emigrated many times throughout the past three generations; her parents are teachers interested in her literacy development; and so on. This is the description of a unique family (as unique as any other family in this world [See Lanteigne & Schwarzer (1997) for another example]); however, the understanding of each child's peculiar language history, family language history, and language communities is the first step in furthering our understanding of their literacy development in general and multiliteracy development in particular.

2

The Text: An In-Depth Analysis of Noa's Literacy Development

Writing Genres: A Working Definition

What are writing genres? Using Halliday's (1975) distinction between *form and function,* a genre is a particular combination of a written *form* used for a particular *function. Form* is defined as the special format that organizes a written piece (a letter, a story, a card, etc.); and *function* is defined as the specific purpose for which writing is done (to complain, to share thoughts, to communicate appreciation, etc.). Therefore, in our daily life we use different forms for different functions. This phenomenon is extremely important in the classroom situation. In recent years, there has been a debate about teaching genres (Carney 1992). A group of Australian linguists, following the basic ideas of Halliday, proposed using direct instruction in order to teach marginalized children conventional genres (Martin 1991). Martin believes that children, especially those in marginalized circumstances, should be directly taught "genres of power," which will contribute to student mobility within the social context. According to Martin's perspective, researchers such as Graves (1983),

Atwell (1987), and Calkins (1986), who are interested in developing literacy through a more holistic approach and investigating all writing genres based on students communicational needs, are not helping marginalized children to access the genres of power. Moreover, Martin asserts that this second group of researchers is perpetuating the students' marginalized situation by avoiding direct instruction of the genres of power. My analysis of Noa's writing genres shows that children can access many more genres when they are offered classroom and home experiences conducive to multiliteracy development. There is no need for direct instruction in order for Noa to investigate different and varied writing genres throughout the year. In terms of the discussion about genres of power, it worries me that some researchers, concerned about empowering marginalized students, have no problem finding the "solution" for them as well as deciding which writing genres they need in order to access social power. I believe that Noa chose most of her writing genres because they were genres of power for her at the time. Moreover, I believe that by letting students investigate different writing genres, they become empowered about the different writing forms available for them as well as the variety of functions for their writings.

Noa Experiments with Writing Genres

Throughout her first year of instruction, Noa investigated twenty-five different writing genres. Some of these writing genres were those more traditionally used in elementary schools (journal writing, spelling preparation, etc.). Noa also investigated and used more unusual genres, such as scientific writing, card writing, and so forth, both at home and in school.

Noa's account shows that children can deal with a different and diverse range of writing genres, even in the first grade. Noa's teacher facilitated the interaction of children with these diverse genres. By this time, I had a clear sense of how to define a *writing genre* in a first grade class, and what is *one written piece* for a first grade student. (For a more detailed explanation, see the appendix). I was also interested in showing the different genres in a chronological format.

Being immersed in the data for a while was a terrifying but crucial step in the process of discovery. From this important experience I was able to find the emergent written themes from the data. Halliday (1979) described three different ways in which language can be learned. According to his ideas, as children use language, they are at the same time immersed in *learning language, learning about language*, and *learning through language*. In examining Noa's writing, it was clear that she experienced *language learning* throughout the year in whatever context or situation that the writing experience happened. However, as I was going over her writings, two very different ways of language learning became differentiated in the various contexts of Noa's learning. In some pieces of Noa's writing, she learned *about* language; language became an *end in itself*. Language as an end in itself took place only in the school setting. For example, Noa wrote fifty-three pieces that were categorized as copying. Copying is a real-life written genre: Writers often copy information from bulletin boards, cards, announcements, and so on. However, all of Noa's writings in this category were a result of copying as a pedagogical device in order to practice "writing": copying from the blackboard, copying from a worksheet into her own handwriting, and so forth. This category included Noa's writing that was written as a copying practice without an authentic purpose.

When Noa was asked to copy from the board and the purpose wasn't for copying as practice for writing, I categorized the writing piece in the other genre. For example, on

Valentine's Day, the teacher wrote several sentences on the blackboard for the children to copy. Noa copied those sentences, but she wrote them in the format of a card. I categorized that writing sample as a card rather than as a copying piece of writing. This categorization issue is very important, because, in many cases, the other categories included pieces that Noa copied from somewhere, but she used them for purposes other than copying. On such occasions, copying became a strategy and was neither an instructional activity nor simply a copying event.

For example, Noa copied the written piece in Figure 2–1 from the blackboard and then illustrated the "story." The story was composed by the students in the class, having in mind a particular sound, in this case /b/.

Figure 2–1. Copying, August 1994

More purposeful writing, which led Noa to learn more about the world, took place in the school setting as well as in the home: she *learned through language;* language became a *means toward an end.* For example, Noa wrote fifty-two pieces that were categorized as journal writing. This category included Noa's writings that were part of a journal assignment or pieces of writing that seem to be written as some kind of diary entry. In these entries, the audience is usually the writer herself, and there is no signature at the end.

According to my research findings, there are numerous ways in which teachers can help students develop multiple writing genres: Teachers can model varied writing genres to children. It is clear from the research findings that Noa's teacher initiated several writing genres and increased Noa's repertoire. For example, in our household, card writing was not a common practice. When the teacher selects reading and writing materials to be modeled in the class, she or he should have in mind the different writing genres available. When students are engaged in discussion about issues related to their reading or writing, teachers should address particular genre-related conventions, such as signature at the end of a letter, dedication at the beginning of a book, the interrelation between writings and diagrams in scientific diagram writing, and so forth. Most importantly, teachers should not underestimate the capability of students to investigate on their own and try as many genres as they choose.

The school setting was often a catalyst for Noa's experiments and inventions in genres that were not available or explored at home. Scientific diagram writing as well as card writing are two good examples of this relationship between home and school.

Noa's teacher introduced scientific diagram writing to the students through experiences related to natural science research. Noa enjoyed the experience, and then she incorporated that genre into her own writing at home while she was playing with other children. In her writings at home, she developed with Sharon (a bilingual Hebrew/English friend) one experiment: They both wrote their own hypotheses and the list of the materials needed, and they made a diagram to exemplify the experiment (Figure 2–2). I

Figure 2–2. Scientific Diagram Writing, March 1995

wonder if this kind of open-ended activity could have taken place in the classroom. (For a fuller description, see Chapter 3, Figure 3–8.)

My interest in Noa's knowledge of written language development raised a number of issues: How many genres did Noa develop during her first year of schooling? Were the genres used differently depending on the language that Noa used? Did the various genres occur in the different settings, and is there a clear distinction between genres that occur at home and genres that occur in school?

More Lessons from Noa's Writing Development

I tried to incorporate into my final categories of analysis all the issues listed above: I developed folders according to the different genres that emerged from the analysis of Noa's written pieces. The genres were categorized as follows: (1) the distinction between language as an end in itself and language as a means toward an end and (2) the context of the writing experience. Most of the genres listed under the category related to language as an end in itself were written in the school setting, while most of the genres listed under the category related to language as a means to an end were written at home or in the school setting. In this first analysis of Noa's genres, I paid attention to the writing genres regardless of the language in which they were written (English, Hebrew, or Spanish).

Noa wrote an astonishing 402 written pieces, which I categorized into twenty-five different genres that developed throughout the eleven months of the study. The first nine genres (boldface in Figure 2–3) correspond to the genres categorized as language as an end in itself, and they were written only in the school setting. Genres coded between

Genre	Total
1. **Copying**	53
2. **Commercial work sheets**	40
3. **Phonics patterns**	25
4. **Spelling test preparation**	19
5. **Spelling test**	11
6. **Fill in the blanks**	8
7. **Sequencing**	5
8. **Sentence completion**	5
9. **Daily oral language**	3
10. Journal writing	52
11. Book writing	27
12. Sentence writing	25
13. Names and label writing	19
14. Book reading/coloring	19
15. Letter writing	12
16. Card writing	11
17. Story writing	11
18. List writing	8
19. Poems and song writing	7
20. Scientific diagram writing	6
21. Signs writing	4
22. Literacy in play	25
23. Recording events	4
24. Note taking from phone	2
25. Receipt	1
Total	402

Figure 2–3. Noa's Writing Genres

the numbers 10 and 25 five are described as language as a means toward an end, with 10 to 21 happening both in school and at home, while 22 to 25 happened only at home.

Following is a more detailed analysis of Noa's writing genres divided into these two main categories:

1. Using language as an end in itself, in the school setting only
2. Using language as a means toward an end, in both home and school

Language as an End in Itself (School Setting Only)

The written pieces listed in Figure 2–4 were used by Noa's teacher in order to teach children how to read and write in a traditional phonics-centered program. These writing genres sometimes are created for school practice and do not exist outside of a school classroom setting; or they exist as

Language as an End in Itself	Total
1. Copying	53
2. Commercial work sheets	40
3. Phonics patterns	25
4. Spelling test preparation	19
5. Spelling test	11
6. Fill in the blanks	8
7. Sequencing	5
8. Sentence completion	5
9. Daily oral language	3
Total	169

Figure 2–4. Language as an End in Itself

real-life genre, but they are used in the classroom without an authentic purpose.

Nine well-known writing genres are identified: copying, commercial work sheets, phonics patterns, spelling test preparation, spelling test, fill in the blanks, sequencing, sentence completion, and daily oral language.

Noa wrote 169 pieces that could be categorized as language as an end in itself. All of these written artifacts are products of a phonic-based curriculum. The largest category is copying and commercial work sheets (93 out of 169). It is interesting to note that some of the genres were used throughout the whole year, while others were condensed to a particular time of the year. Remember, this type of writing was imposed on Noa; she filled in the blanks, she traced the letter, copied the same word three times. Noa reacted to the curricular choices made by the teacher and the writing program she was using. It is clear from the data that phonics patterns were used only between the months of August and December, and spelling test preparation and spelling tests started in January. Those weren't decisions made by the writer, but were determined by the teacher and the curricular program.

I found hard to understand the need to evaluate a first grade student's literacy development nineteen times in only five months. However, Noa had nineteen spelling tests in five months (between January and May). This "developmental practice" of starting phonics instruction, stressing phonics patterns and only after that moving to spelling test preparations and spelling tests, is very common in traditional first grade classes. It is interesting to note that daily oral language (a curricular activity that encourages the teacher to write a daily sentence on the blackboard with a particular mistake that is resolved by the whole class with assistance of the teacher) was used as a strategy for teaching writing by Noa's first teacher in the school (during Noa's first two weeks in the school), while the other teacher used phonics patterns. This difference in early reading approaches suggests that we will encounter a great deal of differences in writing genres developed, while language is treated as an end in itself, depending on curricular programs or teacher preferences throughout the first grade experience.

Language as a Means Toward an End (School and Home Settings)

In this category, I included pieces of writing related to real-life genres. Some of these real-life genres were used for instructional purposes (only at school); some of the writings were initiated at school and were transformed by Noa into meaningful and authentic activities as she chose to bring her own needs and purposes to the writing. Thus, some writings that occurred mostly at home were written as part of real literacy events, as a result of genuine needs.

All the genres in this section could be considered as instructional events only if they lacked a real purpose for the writer. In some classes, the teacher used real-life genres as an end in themselves, solely for the purposes of teaching reading and writing. On the other hand, genres can be viewed as models for children to adopt, even if they are initiated as inauthentic instructional activities. For example, journal writing, scientific diagram writing, and card writing were introduced at school as assignments, many times without a real purpose for the children but rather to fulfill the teacher's requirement. However, when Noa experienced these genres, she assimilated them (Piaget 1971) into her repertoire of genres, and she used them in the home, for play as well as stylistic devices. Noa also accommodated her knowledge to a new genre of writing that she hadn't used before. Noa and her writing were changed by the experience.

Nevertheless, real-life genres occur as part of real-life literacy events in the lives of children. When children have the need to write a note, or to record an event, they do so in the most natural way. Following is the list of the categories related to language as a means toward an end in the home and school settings, using real genres sometimes in authentic ways and other times in inauthentic ways. The last four categories—writing receipts, taking notes, recording events, and literacy in play—happened only in the home setting and as the result of an authentic literacy event.

I describe each of the following categories in detail because I believe they are extremely important in developing authentic writing genre experiences in a first grade class.

Journal Writing This category includes Noa's writings that were part of a journal assignment or pieces of writing that seemed to be written as some kind of diary entry. In these entries, the audience is usually the writer herself, and there is no signature at the end.

Book Writing In this category, I include written pieces that resemble the format and content of a book. These pieces had several pages, with a clear sense of front and back pages. In most of the books, there is a picture on each page and some writing. Sometimes the written piece is only a word, sometimes a sentence, and sometimes a short paragraph. The pieces written in the school setting were generated by a teacher's assignment, while the books written at home were self-generated.

Sentence Writing This category includes Noa's writing of sentences. All of this writing was done as an instructional device to summarize a school activity or as a way to practice some kind of language form, such as possessives, new vocabulary, and so on.

Names and Label Writing In this category, I include written pieces that were a result of the teacher asking the students to draw a picture and to write one word related to the picture. Most of Noa's pieces show her strategy of naming the main event or idea of the picture.

Book Reading/Coloring In this category, I include "books" that were read and colored at school or at home. In most cases, the students read the book with the teacher. Sometimes, the parents read the books to the students at home. Noa read the book by herself at school while she colored the pictures. She read them both in English and in Spanish

Letter Writing This category includes all of Noa's writings that followed the form of a letter: Greetings (Dear _____), the body of the letter with a message to another person, and sometimes a signature.

Card Writing I include in this category communications with the intention to convey greetings or wishes for another person: thank-you notes, happy birthday cards, Valentine cards, and so forth. Cards sometimes share some of the characteristics of a letter, but the main difference between them is that a card conveys wishes and usually does not include events. They also have a different design and format. There is usually a drawing related to the theme of the card, and the paper is folded.

Story Writing This category includes written pieces that are narratives—a series of sentences that convey an experience to a reader. According to Pitcher and Prelinger (1963), there are three conventions in the stories of young writers: formal opening or title, formal closing, and consistent use of past tense. A picture provided by the teacher inspired some of these writing samples.

List Writing In this category, I include all of Noa's writings that were composed as a list. Most of these pieces consist of a series of two or more words written in a column.

Poem and Song Writing This category includes poetry and song writing or other literary pieces. In some pieces, there was a clear attempt to rhyme. The format of the written pieces was also considered in order to decide on the category. Some of the pieces were written in a verselike format, and some were written in the company of a friend.

Scientific Diagram Writing In this category, I include written pieces that show a picture of an object and arrows that point to the different parts of that object. Accompanying the arrows, there are one or two words labeling that particular part of the object. This type of diagram was used mostly in natural sciences projects. Sometimes, the written pieces included a scientific hypothesis for the experiments as well as the list of ingredients needed.

Sign Writing In this category, I include Noa's writing related to a particular incident during the school year in which her class planted some vegetables in the garden. Noa asked the teacher if she could write the signs for the vegetables so the class would know which vegetables were growing where. In this circumstance, this piece of writing became a powerful experience for Noa's literacy development because of its sense of purpose and free choice. Instead of an instructional activity used for the whole class, Noa used the computer to write the signs, and then she illustrated them. (The difference between the categories of name and label writing and sign writing is important. In the first category, the names and labels were used as an assignment to teach writing, while, in the second category, they were used as a real tool and for a real purpose).

Literacy in Play This category includes pieces written during play that do not fit any other clear category. For example, Noa played with some friends, and, while playing, they wrote the rules to the game they were playing.

Recording Events In this category, I include pieces that were written in order to keep a record of an event such as a conversation, the day and hour of a program on the TV, or ideas to share with the class, such as writings about Passover (a Jewish holiday).

Phone Messages In this category, I include pieces written while Noa was speaking on the phone or while she was listening to the answering machine. Most of the notes included the name of a person and the phone number for calling him or her back.

Receipt Writing In this category, I include all written pieces that were generated as receipts by the writer and resembled a receipt in format. They have an amount, a signature, and the name of the article purchased, and there is one copy for the buyer and one for the seller.

Noa wrote 228 written artifacts in eighteen different real-life genres in the school setting and at home (Figure 2–5). Journal writing, the biggest category (52 out of 228), was introduced and used mostly at school. Note that journal writing is a real life genre that was used in class as a real-life activity: for a purpose, to an audience, providing choices to the student as a writer.

Sometimes it's very easy to assign authentic purposes and audiences to pieces written at home. However, it's my intention throughout this book to show that teachers can make a decision as to whether to ensure students' options in order to develop language as a means toward an end. For example, during her first grade year, Noa read and wrote several books as part of her literacy experiences in the class.

Language as a Means Toward an End	Total
10. Journal writing	52
11. Book writing	27
12. Sentence writing	25
13. Names and label writing	19
14. Book reading/coloring	19
15. Letter writing	12
16. Card writing	11
17. Story writing	11
18. List writing	8
19. Poems and song writing	7
20. Scientific diagram writing	6
21. Signs writing	4
22. **Literacy in play**	25
23. **Recording events**	4
24. **Note taking from phone**	2
25. **Receipt**	1
Total	228

Figure 2–5. Language as a Means Toward an End

Sometimes, the activity was contrived: Write one word on each page of the book in order to describe the picture. However, the whole experience was helping to develop the genre of book writing.

As with the categories related to language as an end in itself, some genres were used throughout the year, while others were introduced at a particular time of the year. Because language was treated as a means toward an end, Noa had opportunities to decide when and how to use these genres. For example, Noa wrote seven poems and songs and eleven cards throughout the year. It appears that these genres were used for different reasons throughout the year.

In Figure 2–5, note that the four categories in boldface were the only ones that occurred exclusively at home.

What We Learned from the Analysis of Noa's Texts

Research Your Students' Writings

Many teachers throughout my presentations were overwhelmed by the amount of written pieces that Noa wrote (402) and the variety of genres investigated in first grade (twenty-five genres). One question I am asked every time is, "Do you think Noa wrote more pieces of writing because you were researching her writing development?" There is no question in my mind that Noa wrote more written pieces because she was aware that her father was researching her writing development. Therefore, we may argue that if we research our students writings, we may kill two birds with one stone: We may develop a way for alternative assessment and encourage our students to write more and with a deeper sense of appreciation for their written work.

Develop Different Written Genres

The amount and the diversity of writing genres investigated by a first grader (402 categorized in twenty-five different genres during eleven months) were striking. I think that in many cases teachers and researchers underestimate the possibilities and the realities related to emergent multiliteracy development. Teachers should develop a language curriculum that fosters exploration of varied written genres throughout the school year.

Develop Literacy Activities That Use Language as a Means Toward an End

As teachers, we have the power to determine the amount, quality, and level of genres in our students' writing development. If a teacher treats language as an end in itself and follows a curricular program full of work sheets, spelling test preparations, and spelling tests, then the students are overexposed to a very particular way of viewing and investigating genres. In Noa's case, her teacher was in a borderline position much advocated by certain groups of researchers: She used what is called a "balanced" whole language–phonics approach to literacy development. She taught phonics in a systematic way while she encouraged students to experiment with writing genres such as books, cards, poems, and so on. In Chapter 3, I argue that when Noa wrote using language in authentic activities, as a means toward an end, her literacy developed greatly. On the other hand, when she was exposed to language used as an end in itself, most of the time during phonics-related activities such as work sheets, test preparations, and tests, the development of literacy throughout the year wasn't very clear.

Through Noa's experiences in the school setting, I came to agree with the conclusions from Bob Wortman's research (1991), in which he found that it's difficult to discuss authenticity in terms of activities, but that we should be looking at authenticity from the writer's perspective. In other words, to assess the level of authenticity of a task, we need to analyze it not only from the teacher–adult perspective, but also from the student–child perspective. Children could interpret activities that may seem authentic to teachers as inauthentic, and vice versa.

Develop Kid-Watching Strategies

While Noa was attending first grade, I was very concerned as a father about her learning experience in this particular bilingual class. I believed that Noa wasn't being challenged enough in her class. I thought that she wasn't getting enough exposure to writing and that her experiences with writing were contrived and directed by the teacher, with the teacher as the only audience. By the end of the analysis of Noa's writing genres, I came to realize that Noa explored many different genres in her school experience. My perception of the class as a thoughtful parent without the analysis of Noa's written pieces was different than my analysis of Noa's writing as a researcher dealing with the data. (For a similar experience about research see Schwarzer, Kahn, & Smart [2000].)

3

Tensions in Noa's Literacy Development

While learning about Noa's literacy development I came to realize that there were several tensions related to children developing literacy. In this chapter, I consider different aspects of Noa's literacy development in terms of tensions between two opposing views: tension between language learning as reflected in the concepts of invention and convention (Goodman 1996); tension between settings, especially the roles of school and home; tension in ownership of the writing process related to choice, especially learner's versus teacher's ownership practices; and finally, tension in editing written language, especially the teacher- versus student-centered editing process.

Language Learning: Invention Versus Convention

In an authentic learning experience, two forces begin to work toward each other. One is the force of personal invention. The other is the force of social convention (Good-man 1990; Whitmore & Crowell 1994). In Noa's literacy development, this tension is clear. Most of Noa's writings were related to the category of language as an end in itself; Noa did not invent new forms of writing. She followed a very strict routine of performing according to social convention. In these writing samples, it is impossible to see any inventions, and therefore to perceive any development. Two examples (one from August [Figure 3–1] and the other from May [Figure 3–2]) were written in school as assignments.

In these examples, there is no sense of development, because the assignments themselves demanded only the conventional form and not any invention on the part of the child. Using language totally free of errors is not an effective way to perceive development. Miscues are the window to the reading process (Goodman et al. 1987), and, thus, invented spelling is the window to the writing process.

Noa was able to fill in the blanks or follow this type of assignment without any difficulty from the first days of class; she filled in the work sheets quickly and then waited for the other children to be done. Looking back at dozens of these written pieces, I am coming to the conclusion that, at least for Noa, they were not necessary, challenging, or even developmentally appropriate. On the contrary, they were "busy work," time to use writing without any other purpose than to follow directions, and work by herself. I often wonder what could have happened to Noa's writing development if the teacher had given Noa more opportunities to explore writing assignments using language as a means toward an end.

Opposite to this lack of development throughout the months of the study, other genres developed in a much

Figure 3–1. Tensions Between Invention and Convention: Language as an End in Itself, August 1994

Noa

Homework 🙂

January 17, 1995

The dog had a frend.
I mad a cake.
I like to make things.
I like to bake.
ther are docks in the lake.

Write each word 5 times.
Choose 5 words. Write a
sentence for each word.

doy   cake
log   bake
hag   make
fog   wake
jog   lake

1. dog dog dog dog dog
2. log log log log log
3. hog hog hog hog hog
4. fog fog fog fog fog
5. jog jog jog jog jog

1. cake cake cake cake cake
2. bake bake bake bake bake
3. make make make make make
4. wake wake wake wake wake
5. lake lake lake lake lake

Figure 3–2. Tensions Between Invention and Convention:
Language as an End in Itself, May 1995

more noticeable way. In Figures 3–3 and 3–4, I show two journal entries that demonstrate a clear sense of Noa's literacy development. In this case, the tensions between invention and convention can be appreciated clearly.

The first journal entry from August (see Figure 3–3) needs to be "translated" into conventional English writing for the reader, while the second entry (see Figure 3–4) is clear enough that it does not need any translation.

Following is a list of issues that Noa understood in May that were not clear in August:

1. Capitalization at the beginning of the entry ("On Mother's Day")
2. The correct use of the possessive ("Mother's Day")
3. Capitalization of the date and its proper position
4. There are forty-six conventional spellings in this fifty-four-word entry. The few inventions include "unduer" for *under*; "wen" for *when*; "now" for *know*; "heer" for *here*; "si" for *is*; and "anuther" for *another*. Dad and

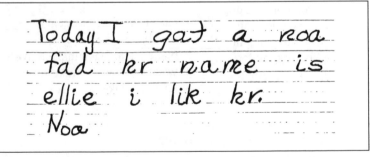

Figure 3–3. Tensions Between Invention and Convention: Language as a Means Toward an End, August 1994. *Translation: Today I got a new friend. Her name is Ellie. I like her.*

May 15, 1995

On Mother's Day
my Dad called my Mom
and my Mom came
my Dad hid me unduer
the bed wen my Mom came
and I said Mom you nou
it su Mother's Day so her
is a card and then I gave
my Mom a nather card
and then I gave her.
the present.

Figure 3–4. Tensions Between Invention and Convention:
Language as a Means Toward an End, May 1995

Mom are capitalized. Moreover, according to Wilde's
(1992) categories of analysis for invented spelling,
Noa's spellings are close to conventional.

Invention and convention are two important compo-
nents of literacy development. The data provide insight
about the lack of invention in all of the material provided
by the teacher to Noa in order to learn about language. On
the other hand, activities that treated language as a means
toward an end, show tensions between these two forces
and their development throughout the year. These tensions
provided Noa with opportunities to explore written language, which influences knowledge of the writing systems
and development.

One extremely important activity that developed
Noa's writing profoundly was journal writing. Noa did
fifty-two entries of journal writing. One of them, a special winter holiday journal, was twenty-five pages long.
The journal used by Noa's teacher was not a dialogue
journal (Peyton & Read 1990), but mostly a diary in
which events were described and recorded. Noa liked
writing journal entries a lot. She enjoyed using the computer to write her journal entries, and she was very glad
when the teacher understood what she wrote. I feel that
journal writing was one of the most successful and powerful teaching experiences that Noa used throughout the
year, both at school and at home. As was stated earlier in
this chapter, in this particular category there is a clear
sense of development from her first entry in August to
her last entry in May.

Another aspect of Noa's inventions throughout the year
is related to her wondering about language. I videotaped
Noa while she was writing the example in Figure 3–5 on the
computer. As she was writing, I came to realize that Noa
used a period to separate the list of words and the sentence

1. cat cat cat cat cat. the cat is fat.
2. hat hat hat hat. the hat shop.
3. that that that that. That is big.
4. rat rat rat rat. The rat hotel is big.
5. bat bat bat bat bat. The bat flew out of the cave.
6. had had had had.
7. mad mad mad mad mad.
8. sad sad sad sad sad.
9. Dad Dad Dad Dad Dad.
10. bad bad bad bad bad.

Figure 3–5. Tensions Between Invention and Convention: Language Learning, May 1995

that followed. In other instances, capitalization was used only to start the sentence and not to start the series of words.

The following is the transcription of our conversation (translated from Hebrew):

David: Why did you write this (pointing at the period) after cat cat cat?

Noa: Because it is the end of the sentence.

David: So why don't you use a capital letter at the beginning of cat cat cat, but you use a capital letter at the beginning of "The cat is fat"?

Noa: (Silence) . . . The first cat cat cat is . . . (pause) is to practice, is for the teacher. The other (pointing to "The cat is fat") says something.

David: Mmm?

Noa: Cat cat cat, see! It's nothing. The cat is fat, that's something!!!

Noa shares a good sense of the convention of a sentence: It starts with a capital letter and ends with a period, but, most importantly, the writer writes it to say something and not to practice. She knows that the lists of the same words written as homework are for the teacher and do not serve any purpose but practice.

I end this section about tension between invention and convention by sharing with you a new understanding I learned while I analyzed Noa's writing. For Noa, writing is a transactional process (Rosenblatt 1978). In my study, Noa's understanding of the writing process developed throughout the year during her acts of writing. While she was writing, not only was she producing outputs; moreover, she was transacting with herself through the writing process. Noa's study of language as a means toward an end provides evidence that writing for a meaningful purpose became a catalyst for her writing development.

Tension Between Home and School

As a researcher, it would be very easy to make a dichotomy between school and home, showing the home setting as good, authentic, and challenging, and the school setting as inadequate, inauthentic, and unchallenging. As Fagan (1995) writes,

> The school and the community often encompass different social relationships. . . . School literacy was perceived by the respondents as being sequential and vertical; that is, its development was expected to occur over a 12-year period . . . The study's participants associated community literacy with group interaction, sharing, and short-term gratification. Community literacy was guided by its meaning and function in the lives of adults and their children. (260)

In Noa's case, there is a clear sense of tension between her writing samples written at home and those written in school. I am trying to highlight both the dichotomies as well as the successful attempts of bridging between these two important parts of Noa's life. Noa's writing in school became more redundant and less expressive over time. She is more careful about her spellings in school than she is at home when she is writing a story or an idea that she is trying to convey. This tension is very clear in the genre of book writing, as seen in the samples of two books written in the different contexts (Figures 3–6 and 3–7).

Figure 3–6 shows the first page of a book written collaboratively between Noa and Dana (a monolingual English speaking child whose mother is a bilingual Hebrew/English speaker) at home. Figure 3–7 shows four pages of a book written in school.

As the reader can see, there are many differences between the book written at home and the one written in school. In the book written at home, Dana and Noa are trying to represent the form of a first page of a children's book: the author, the illustrator, and so on. They are using the conventional format of "Pictures by Noa" in the same way that it will appear in a book: "Illustrations by such and such." As can be appreciated, the spellings of the words are invented and, in many ways, are impossible to read without a "translation." In the book written in school, Noa seems to be very careful about her spelling, but there is no sense of risk taking and exploration of prior knowledge brought to the writing process. In this book, her first page is only " 'Rain' by Noa."

Noa wrote twenty-seven books during her first-grade experience. This experience was of great value for her writing development, especially the books that she chose to write because she had a real audience and a clear purpose.

On the other hand, the school setting was often a

Figure 3–6. Tensions Between Home and School: Book Writing at Home, August 1994. *Translation: (Title) Colorful Colors. (First column) Colors and words by Noa. (Second column) From Noa and Dana. (Third column) Pictures by Dana.*

Figure 3–7. Tensions Between Home and School: Book Writing at School, Undated

catalyst for Noa's experiments and inventions in genres that were not available or explored at home. Scientific diagram writing as well as card writing are two good examples of this tension.

Noa's teacher introduced scientific diagram writing to the students through experiences related to natural science research. Noa enjoyed the experience, and then she incorporated that genre into her own writing at home while she was playing with other children. In her writings at home, she developed with Sharon (a bilingual Hebrew/English friend) one experiment: They both wrote their own hypotheses and the list of the materials needed, and they made a diagram to exemplify the experiment (Figure 3–8). I wonder if this kind of open-ended activity could have taken place in the classroom.

There were many literacy events in play that took place in the home, but none at school. It is almost as if Noa understood that school is for business and only at home can she play with literacy.

Following is a description of a multilingual literacy event in play:

Three Israeli families and Noa's family are sitting in the living room drinking coffee. The children decide to play with the adults, and start asking everyone what they would like to drink (in Hebrew). The adults respond, and Noa writes the list shown in Figure 3–9.

After they serve the tea, Noa comes back for the payment. She writes one receipt and the duplicate; she makes a move over the paper that resembles the movement that store owners do when they "swipe" the credit card, and then she asks me to sign twice (Figure 3–10). Then she says in Hebrew, "This is your copy, sir!" Everyone laughs.

It is very important to notice that literacy in play did not happen at all in the school setting. Noa did not have even one opportunity to use literacy while she was playing in the class.

Noa is very willing to accept school conventions. She enjoys playing and discovering the conventions related to schooling. She is very successful in the school setting, but it provides her with limited challenges. Noa enjoys conforming to schools rules and activities. If she found a new way to play with a school drill, she would try that. For example, Noa found that when the teacher asked her to copy a word

I need 2 # zip
lock bags and
in the zip
lock bags
I need sum
wadr in it

I think that
the tumadow
wil last bekus
befor you aet
the tumalow
you haf to
wosh it.

sum I need
wodr 2 zip
in it lock
bags

banana

Figure 3–8. Tensions Between Home and School: The
Assimilation of a New Genre, March 1995. *Translation: (Top) I
need two zip lock bags and in the zip lock bags I need some water
in it. (Middle) I think that the tomato will last because before you
eat the tomato you have to wash it. (Bottom) A picture of two zip-
lock bags, one with a piece of tomato and one with a piece of
banana. Arrows point out both elements.*

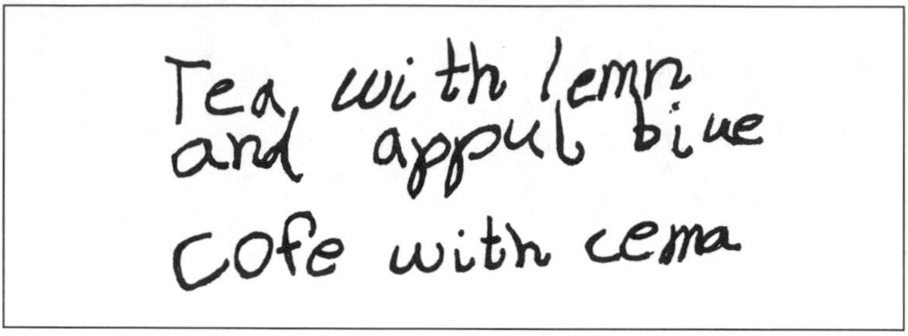

Figure 3–9. Tensions Between Home and School: Literacy in Play, March 1995. *Translation: Tea with lemon and apple pie, coffee with cream.*

five times and then write a sentence with some of the words in the list, it was fun to use the computer. Therefore, she used the "inauthentic" assignment and then converted it into an authentic one for herself. She was no longer copying words and creating sentences; she was learning how to use the computer.

When she was not able to create a meaningful purpose for her writing, she would do exactly what she was expected to do. Language as an end in itself, especially as part of reading instruction in school, became a playful theme for Noa, although it was irrelevant to her multiliteracy development. However, language as a means toward an end was a much more challenging writing experience for Noa, and there are clear data to support her development during the year. Noa knew that, to play the school game, it was better to write a very short book, sentence, or word, making sure that the writing was conventional. At home, she knew that the name of the game was different. Therefore, she took risks and developed different types of books, ones that were richer in themes and invented spellings. My concern as a parent and as a researcher is that Noa may get the idea that, at school,

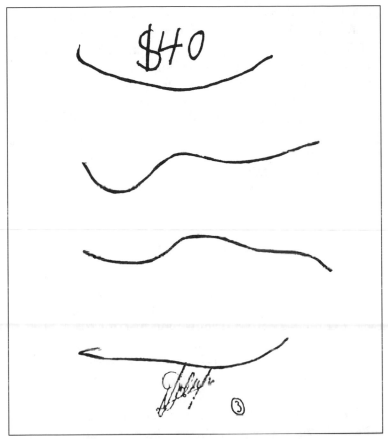

Figure 3–10. Tensions Between Home and School: Literacy in Play, Continued

you only learn things that you already know. In school, Noa performs only at the level of expectations the setting has created: Write conventionally, keep it simple, don't take risks, form is more important than function. However, there is very little challenge in this environment for Noa and children like her. As I finish this research, I wonder what could have happened if Noa had been challenged in her multiliteracy development? How much more knowledgeable could she have been by the end of the year? How could she have developed a better sense of learning in school?

Tensions in Editing: Who Decides and Controls the Process?

In this section, I discuss a very central issue in early literacy development: editing. Many educators think that it is necessary to edit every single mistake a student makes in order to eradicate those mistakes. Others think that there is no need to relate or discuss with students issues related to their editing, because they will do it by themselves. It is my opinion that students should be given the opportunity to reflect on their own mistakes and see them as resources for their development. Noa's teacher corrected many of Noa's writings during the year. Figure 3–11 shows a literacy event that captures the difficulty of editing.

I want to highlight how Noa not only copied the teacher's correction, but also tried to assimilate and accommodate the teacher's information, especially about spelling. The teacher asked Noa to write a story about the class pets: the guinea pigs, Mr. Rose and Crystal. After Noa wrote the story, the teacher corrected it, writing the corrections above Noa's writing. Figure 3-11 is the story written by Noa and corrected by the teacher.

Noa follows the teacher's suggestion to type the correct

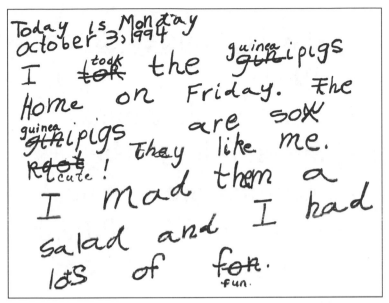

Figure 3–11. Tensions Between Student–Teacher-Centered Editing, October 1994

story on the computer. Figure 3–12 shows the result of Noa's typing. This piece was never corrected or revised again.

It is clear what was going on in Noa's mind as she was rewriting this piece. In her first attempt, she wrote "ginipig," representing the sounds in appropriate ways. When the teacher corrected the piece, she crossed out the first three letters of Noa's attempt. Then she wrote above it "guinea." In rewriting her piece, Noa wrote "guineaipigs." Should the teacher have been more careful when she corrected a student? I think that is a simplistic solution.

In my opinion, Noa's construction of the word *ginipigs* followed English orthographic patterns. In addition, Noa is concerned with the concept that guinea pig is two words that correspond to one animal in real life. However, because

> Today is Monday October
> 3, 1994
> I took the guineaipigs
> home on Friday. The
> guineaipigs are so cute!
> They like me. I mad them
> a salad and I had lots of
> fun.

Figure 3–12. Tensions Between Student–Teacher-Centered Editing, Continued

no discussion took place during the teacher's editing to differentiate between the two strategies used in English orthography, Noa copied and created a third option. Noa's second attempt ("guineaipigs") is, in my opinion, worse than her first meaningful attempt ("ginipigs")*. I think that this vignette about editing has a powerful message for teachers that believe in this type of correction: Children will assimi-

---

*Since it is an attempt made by Noa to please the teacher without fully understanding the correction. Noa was encouraged to replace the words without thinking.

late corrections, sometimes in ways that are not expected, with interesting results.

There is another way to approach the issue of editing, and that is through the power of the genres themselves. Noa's poem and song-writing genre was very important to her. During Noa's writing of a song, she used, for the one and only time during the whole first grade, the concept of going from a first draft to a final draft. I think that Noa realized that, in order to write a song or a poem, she needed to attempt more than one aesthetic option for her writing. She used a paper to write and then erased part of her first draft (Figure 3–13). Only then did she copy it into the final draft (Figure 3–14).

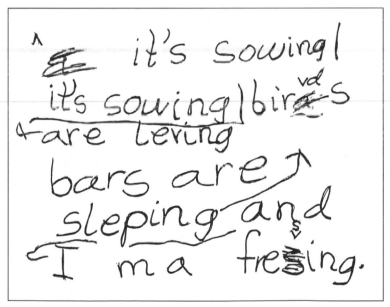

Figure 3–13. Tensions Between Student–Teacher-Centered Editing: Genre Influences—First Draft, December 1994

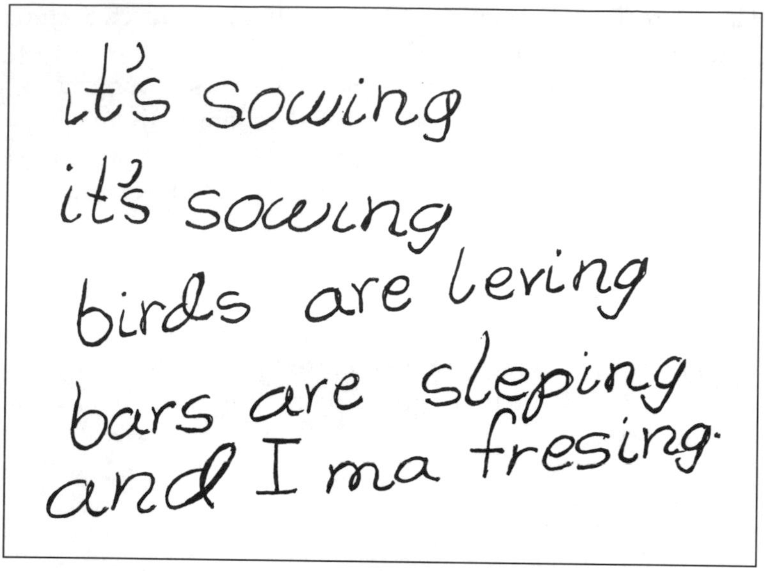

it's sowing
it's sowing
birds are leving
bars are sleping
and I ma fresing.

Figure 3–14. Tensions Between Student–Teacher-Centered Editing: Genre Influences—Final Draft, December 1994

To finish this chapter, I quote Hall (1991), who writes about his concerns regarding literacy development:

> Whereas Ferreiro and Teberosky (1982) are interested in how young children view literacy as an object of knowledge, Harste, Woodward and Burke (1984) are concerned with how children view literacy as a process. They focus on how children understand literacy in a social sense—not just on how print works, but also on the where, what, why and when of literacy in all its manifestations. (6)

It was my intention throughout the entire analysis of these data to integrate both views about Noa's writings. In

Chapter 2, in the analysis of Noa's genres according to forms and functions, I researched her writing primarily as an object of study. In this chapter, I integrated the view of writing as an object of study as well as writing as a social process. In my opinion, only the integration of both aspects gives us a powerful picture of early literacy development.

4

To Be or Not to Be Multiliterate? That's the Question!

This is the most important question every educator in the world should ask: Is being multiliterate an asset or a problem? Should we even strive for multiliteracy development as one of our curricular goals in early childhood education? Many teachers (among them, Noa's teacher) feel that multi-literacy is an important asset only for a few bright children. They do encourage multicultural practices in their classes, but, on the other hand, they only foster literacy development in English, even with multilingual children.

Now, it was expected that Noa, coming from a truly multilingual family, being imbedded in many multilingual communities, and being aware of being studied for "Daddy's book," would have written many more pieces in languages other than English. However, after reviewing Noa's writings, I found that she wrote less than 10 percent of her overall pieces in languages other than English. This is a major finding: Even children coming from multilingual families, living in multilingual communities, and being aware of their parents desires and commitment to multilingualism, hardly write in languages other than English. It looks as if the sociopolitical atmosphere of the United States that openly supports legislation for English-only schools; that prefers English as a Second Language instruction over bilingual education in states such as California; that accepts bilingual education programs in elementary schools but does not allow them in middle schools, such as in the state of Texas sends very clear hidden messages to our bilingual and multilingual students: English is much more important than any other languages you may use at home.

I will describe in detail the few writings that happened in languages other than English and build on them in order to create a repertoire of tools and ideas to be used during reading and language arts instruction in schools.

Writing in Different Languages

One of the basic goals of this book is to present a first grader's journey into multiliteracy. Figure 4–1 is a chart listing the number of writing pieces done in different languages during the research. Noa wrote 369 pieces of

Genre/ Month of Year	July	Aug	Sept	Oct	Nov	Dec	Jan	Feb	Mar	Apr	May	Total
1. English		31	33	42	41	31	40	32	39	43	25	369
(12 undated)												
2. Spanish	5		1		4	1	2	1	11	2		27
3. Hebrew				1		2		1		1	1	6
Total	5	31	34	43	45	34	42	34	50	46	26	402

Figure 4–1. Writing in Different Languages

writing in English, only twenty-seven pieces in Spanish (although this was a bilingual class!), and the astonishing six pieces in Hebrew. It is obvious from Figure 4–1 that English was the language Noa wrote in most. As mentioned earlier, less than 10 percent of her writing was in a language other than English.

It was a big disappointment for me, as a researcher and as Noa's father, to see her writing development mostly in one language. Following is an in-depth analysis of Noa's writing in languages other than English.

Writing in Spanish

One disturbing aspect of this analysis of Noa's writing is that she wrote only twenty-seven pieces in Spanish, although she studied in a bilingual class. It is important to remember the particular understanding of bilingual education in Noa's first-grade experience. The classroom teacher is a bilingual educator and shares her class with a bilingual paraprofessional that comes once a day for two hours. During those hours, the class is divided into the Spanish group and the English group. During this time, children are taught how to read and write in English or Spanish, depending on the group they were assigned. Noa was the only dominant-English-speaking student allowed to join the "Spanish group" once a week, owing to my insistence. From interviews with Noa's teacher, it is clear that she believed that becoming a balanced bilingual in two languages was a long process. Moreover, she quoted research that showed it takes seven years to become bilingual (Cummins 1984).

When I raised the concern that Noa was not reading and writing in Spanish, the teacher explained to me that she believes that children should learn how to be able to speak a language first, and only then are they allowed to read or write it. Although the teacher's reaction is not unusual, there is evidence that children can learn two languages without setting up such restrictions. Biliteracy development can be easy to foster in a biliterate community (Goodman et al. 1979). Furthermore, the work of researchers such as Moll and Diaz (1987) offers supportive views about biliteracy development. They found that students could deal with reading and writing in a second language, even at the beginning of their oral development in that language. Speaking is not necessarily a prerequisite for literacy development, especially in a second language.

While I was conducting this research, I started to consider the real purpose of Noa's bilingual class. Originally, I had thought that the teacher was interested in a two-way bilingual class, in which the English speakers learned Spanish and the Spanish speakers learned English. To the contrary, this class was organized into two groups. The Spanish group was taught by a paraprofessional, while the classroom teacher taught the English group. This arrangement did not create an atmosphere conducive to the development of biliteracy. Even after Noa joined the Spanish group once a week, she was viewed as a "special case," and only because of her "success" in the development of English did the teacher allow her to join the Spanish group.

Noa's teacher said,

> Noa is a very special child. . . . She is very good with languages, that's why she can join the Spanish group . . . for her this is a very good experience, but not all the children are as bright as Noa.

Noa had learned a lot of oral-receptive Spanish. She understands some of the conversations that my wife and I conduct in Spanish and so on. Regarding her literacy development in Spanish, she can now determine whether a text is written in English or in Spanish. The following series of events show Noa's literacy development in Spanish during her first-grade experience.

In July 1995, we traveled to Argentina. On the plane, the flight attendants offered the passengers newspapers in Spanish. Noa asked me, "Daddy, do they write Spanish in English?"

At the beginning I was not able to understand why she was asking this strange question. But after reflecting on Noa's language experiences, I realized that, in Noa's experience with Hebrew and English, different languages have different orthographies. Her expectation was that Spanish would have yet another orthography. In the midst of the flight, Noa began to realize that Spanish and English shared a similar orthography. Noa was building an intuitive understanding about how writing systems work.

At the end of the year, I asked Noa's Spanish teacher how Noa was doing in Spanish. The following is my translation of the conversation that took place in Spanish:

> This last week I gave Noa some stories to copy from another student while the other students were taking a test. While she was copying the stories, she seemed to be very upset about something. I asked her what was wrong, and she told me, "Mrs. R., this is not right; J. made a mistake; you don't write 'del'; you write 'de el'."

Noa knew enough Spanish to feel comfortable confronting her fellow student's writing and to provide evidence of her own invention. In Spanish, the correct form is "del," which is a contraction of the preposition "de" and the masculine article "el." However, in other places, "de él" is separated, such as in "¿De quién es este lápiz? De él." ("Whose pencil is this? It is his.") In this case, "de él" means "his" (the preposition "de" and the pronoun "él.") I think that these two stories give the reader a sense that Noa was wondering about and developing literacy in Spanish.

Of the twenty-seven pieces of Spanish writing, Noa wrote only two of them at home. The rest of her writing was done in the school setting. Twenty-five out of twenty-seven pieces written in Spanish were copied from the blackboard, and they are best described as phonics patterns.

Writing in Hebrew

To everybody's surprise, Noa wrote only six pieces of writing in Hebrew. Noa knows much more Hebrew than she realizes, but she adopted her school perspective about literacy learning: Literacy can be learned only by drills and practice and based on "formal instruction." In many of our conversations throughout the year, Noa explained to me that she was not writing in Hebrew because she did not know how. However, when she attempted to write some Hebrew, it was clear that she knew some of the letters sounds and the graphic shapes of the letters, and she understood Hebrew directionality. With pressure from her parents, she attempted some writings on Hebrew of her own. Noa knows that our family intends to go back to Israel, and many times she was concerned about the fact that she does not know "how to read and write in Hebrew." All of our efforts to tell Noa that she knows how to read and write in Hebrew, that she needs just to try, were in vain. In her opinion, we need to formally teach her how to read and write, and without this "direct instruction," she will not be able to learn it. Therefore, some of the Hebrew entries are related to a Hebrew workbook for children that we have at home.

Figure 4–2 shows one entry of Noa's writing in the

Figure 4–2. Writing in Hebrew, December 1994

workbook. In this piece of writing, Noa was reading and writing in the Hebrew workbook. The workbook focused on the written forms "ba" and "na," two syllables traditionally used to start teaching Hebrew. Noa was engaged in her work until I asked her if she knew how to write *banana* (a word that does not appear in the workbook). Noa tried her own invention (bottom right in Figure 4–2). Noa wrote banana using invented spelling.

Hebrew is mostly a syllabic written language. Most Hebrew words are written without representing the vowel sounds. The Hei, H, /h/ sound (the second letter from the left in Figure 4–1 in Noa's writing) is used most of the time in a final position when the word ends in an open vowel. It is also an indicator of a feminine noun. This is the way that the word *banana* would have been written in English transliteration: B N N H. Noa wrote the word *banana* in her invented spelling, transliterated to English in this way: B H N N H. She used an extra H in the middle of the word *banana*. The type of invented spelling described before is not an unusual one for an Israeli child learning Hebrew in Israel. Noa explained to me that she included the extra H to take the place of the sound <a> (which is not represented in conventional written Hebrew). She also explained, "I put this (pointing at the H) because that's always at the end of words in Hebrew." From this example, we can observe that Noa had more knowledge about the Hebrew writing system than she was able to recognize.

In the context of her multiliteracy development, she perceives her Hebrew writing development only as the result of direct instruction. She is immersed in Hebrew literature, letters, lists, and so on, but she does not perceive these experiences as a resource for her literacy development in Hebrew.

Noa's use of Hebrew in some ways was affected by her family experiences. She knows that our family situation is usual to the university professors in Israel. She is aware of the fact that it is going to take her a while until she will be able to read and write at the same level of an Israeli child her same age. On the other hand, she understands the advantages of knowing how to read and write in English and the temporary nature of the problem. Noa knows that after a few months in Israel, she will be able to read and write as well as any of her classmates. These are her comments about this issue:

> May 1995: "I know that it is going to take me a while until I will be able to read and write in Hebrew like my friends in Israel. . . . But they don't know how to read and write in English like I do."

Noa is not worried about her Hebrew development. She knows that it is going to take time, but she knows she is going to be as successful as other people in her family history have been before. Knowing one's family literacy history seems to be a key point in any writer's literacy development.

Noa is aware of the impact that an audience has on the development of a new language. She clearly stated that there is a need for a silent period (Krashen 1990). But on the other hand, she also indicates a need for an audience with which she can check her hypotheses about language.

Noa's Journey Revisited

I think Noa's account tells us a lot about the unspoken sociopolitical message of many schools in this country, even bilingual programs: Reading and writing in English is very important, it is the key for school success, while reading and writing in languages other than English is "good" but is left to be developed by the student's family or the local communities. I think Noa's account is showing us that, even under the most supportive family environment (two Hebrew teachers, doing research on their own child's second languages development, having extensive exposure to children's books, etc.) and language communities (participating in the local Jewish community, participating in the local Israeli community, etc.), Noa believes she needs to be taught Hebrew and Spanish formally in order to be able to read or write it. Moreover, she does not seem to view the importance of her family and community languages in her literacy development. I am often asked whether I believe that Noa's case study can help us understand other children's literacy and multiliteracy development. I can hardly imagine a child developing multiliteracy under better conditions than was Noa. And, even then, she wrote only a few pieces of writing in languages other than English. I can assume that children living in families that may have mixed feelings about using their first language with their children, less exposure to written materials in the home language, and an unclear commitment to the improvement and maintenance of the home language may end up writing even less than Noa.

I believe that when children come to our classrooms speaking languages other than English, we should commit ourselves to the development of the gifts they're bringing with them from their homes. Teachers' perspectives on this issue seem to be crucial to the development or the loss of the home language (as discussed in Chapter 5). Teachers should become especially interested in those children and in the ways that the class and the school may be able to support and enhance their home language development. I believe we should understand that the children and their families are coming to the first-grade experience with mixed signals. Many times, Noa heard people on the supermarket line or on our family vacations telling us how important it is to speak English to our children, because we are in an English-speaking country. Some parents may have discussions about this with psychologists or teachers that believe parents should speak English at home in order to help their children with better transition to an English-only curriculum.

On the other hand, older children of the family or relatives in the countries of origin want their grandchildren or cousins to be able to speak the home languages, and they place a lot of value on maintaining the home languages. Therefore, teachers should assume a proactive role: They should explain to both children and family why it is important to improve their first languages. I often speak to groups of parents and teachers concerned with this issue, and I use an interesting metaphor. I believe that each child that comes to my class and was exposed to another language has a raw diamond in their hands. We can help the family and the community cut and polish the diamond so it will shine, or we can have the children bury and lose the raw diamond in the mud, and it will never shine. It is my opinion that Noa's teacher did not think it was part of her duty to foster Noa's literacy development in Hebrew.

5

Lessons Learned from Noa's Journey

For many years, there has been a "debate" surrounding bilingualism in early childhood. McLaughlin (1984) outlined three basic positions about early bilingualism: the maximalist position, the minimalist position, and the intermediate position. I add the multiliteracy position to this debate. In my opinion, researchers of this topic underestimate the capabilities of children to develop more than one written and spoken language. They appear to be afraid that learning two written and spoken languages will confuse the child. Noa's journey shows that she ponders many complex issues related to all the written and spoken languages in her life, and her questions have a positive impact on her multiliteracy development.

There are four basic ways to deal with students' native languages in the school setting: to forbid them, to allow them, to maintain them, or to foster them.

To forbid multiliteracy development is, in some ways,

to ignore children's home languages. Many teachers are unaware of their students' home languages. In most cases, they perceive as their main job the fostering of English literacy development. By doing so, de facto, they are forbidding children the opportunity to acquire an important gift: their home language(s).

Other teachers allow students to use their native languages in the school setting. If children are using Spanish during recess, that's OK. If one child translates to another during class time, that's OK, too. However, the use of the home languages is allowed only for the purpose of teaching or developing the English language.

In a few other settings, schools and school districts, under a lot of pressure from minority parents, agree to create classes or afternoon clubs in order to maintain students' home languages. In these cases, most of these classes happen after school or as extracurricular activities and they are taught, not by the regular classroom teacher, but by a "special" teacher who knows the language. Of course, minority children are segregated during these classes, because only the same language minority children participate in these activities.

Fostering of early multiliteracy development in the mainstream class by the monolingual teacher seems, by far, the most radical and important option. To foster students' multiliteracy, monolingual classroom teachers must show interest in children's home languages, those both read and written in the house. Teachers should inquire about this, not just as part of the home language survey or for the district's needs, but also in order to help them find someone in the school and/or home communities that will be able foster the students' languages within the classroom setting.

How Do Monolingual Teachers Foster Early Multiliteracy Development?

Following are some *misconceptions* about early multiliteracy development.

Monolingual Language Teachers Cannot Foster Multiliteracy Because They Are Not Multiliterate Themselves.

You do not need to be bilingual or multilingual in order to show real appreciation for students' home languages. Ask them about family members and the languages they speak, read, or write; tell them about yourself and your desire to include in the class as many languages as possible; explain to them why it is important that you and the others in the class foster these languages; keep a chart in your class showing the names of your students, their birthplaces or places of origin, and the languages they speak, read, and write. Keep another chart showing the names of people in the school communities and the languages they speak, read, and write. You can also keep a map with the name of the students and community members and their countries of origin.

Classroom Teachers Are the Only Ones That Can Teach Languages in the Classroom.

If classroom teachers create a multiliteracy learning community, parents, siblings, elders, paraprofessionals, custodians, cafeteria staff, and so forth can become involved in the students' multiliteracy development. Because literacy is socially constructed (Goodman 1990), creating a multiliteracy learning community seems to be a very workable solution for monolingual teachers. As a monolingual teacher, you cannot actually teach students' home languages. However, you can create a multiliteracy learning community in which literacy in different languages will flourish under your guidance. Your input in setting the community to work is crucial: You need to talk first to the students about the importance of their home languages, then with their parents in order to ask for their time and support, and then with the school at large to gain the needed resources for this curricular change.

Teachers That Do Not Know How to Write in Languages Other Than English Cannot Foster Writing in the Students' Home Languages.

A major role as a teacher trying to foster multiliteracy development in the class is to provide students with a rich multiliterate print environment. As teachers, we know that young children learn a lot about literacy from the print environment in which they live. As teachers fostering multiliteracy, we should create a rich print environment in children's home languages: We may ask their parents to bring in books in their first languages, or empty bottles, containers, and other objects containing print; we may ask a custodian who speaks and reads in one of the home languages to write its alphabet. These may seem like minor efforts, but they will have a major impact on children's perspectives about the value of their first language.

If Teachers Do Not Know Students' Home Languages, They Cannot Assess Students' Language Proficiency in Those Languages.

This may sound awkward, but you *do not need to know* Hebrew in order to determine whether the child can read it fluently. If the child stumbles over every other word, or looks at you as if asking for help, or reads in a monotone, these are likely signs that the child is not very comfortable reading in the home language. Ask questions about his or her reading, ask what the story is about, and try to see whether he or she can show you a word that repeats itself in the same text. (Even if you do not know Chinese, you may be able to recognize the same character in two different places. If they are not the same, there may be an explanation, or you may assume that the child is not able to read the text.) If available, use the parents or another teacher/paraprofessional as a resource; a university in which the language of the child is taught; a consulate or an embassy of the child's country of origin; or a local church or Sunday school where that language is spoken. Knowing students' literacy development in their first languages is important in order to be able to choose which activities may be most suitable for them.

Teachers That Do Not Know Students' Home Languages Cannot Help to Foster Them.

As language teachers, we must remember that language learning is language learning. What is good for a first grade child, in order to foster English as a first language is, in most cases, good for the same child to foster any other first language. Use any teaching and learning strategy for developing English literacy in order to further multiliteracy development.

Depending on the children's proficiency in their first languages, as assessed by the teacher (see the previous discussion), there are many strategies available. At the beginning level, the teacher may ask someone from the students' language community to start a weekly dialogue journal with the students. A dialogue journal is a weekly letter between two or more people that are trying to maintain a written conversation. The teacher's role is to get it started, to explain to the adult that the written conversation should be kept simple and predictable, and that the adult should respond to the understandable message and try to correct any mistakes made by the children by using the same utterance in their response but in its correct form. Once in a while, the teacher may ask the students to bring in their dialogue journals and read something to her. She may even write, in English, something to both parties to encourage their conversation.

If you happen to have in your class or in your grade level more than one child speaking the same first language, you may think about creating a writing workshop specially designed to foster multiliteracy. Students may read a translated version of the book you are reading to the whole class, or another book in their home language that is related to the theme you are teaching. You may encourage them to participate in a bilingual writing workshop in English and in their home language. You may want to start a book cycle based on a book or a theme you are teaching to the whole class; students may have discussions in English while they read the book in their first language, and sometimes they may have discussions lead by community members that speak the same language. You may also consider reading a book by a famous author from their country that has been translated into English, and some children may be able to read this author's book in their native tongue. You may lead discussions about the differences between the original book and its translation.

Monolingual Teachers Are Exempted from Learning Their Own Families' Home Languages.

Monolingual teachers should explore their own home languages. As with most issues in language education, modeling is an important part of language development. Many teachers come from immigrant families: some from French backgrounds, some from German ones, others from Italian ones. I believe that teachers should explore their own home languages and, by doing so, provide a model for students to follow. We can start by looking up our last names on the Internet and seeing what languages and countries have World Wide Web pages; we can interview older family members and ask them if they remember or know about a particular country, province, or area from which the family came, and then research what languages are spoken and written in those areas; we can research some of our family's traditional foods and their names, which sometimes are still used in the home language.

Once we discover what language or languages were spoken in our homes, we may want to learn how to write our own names in the home language writing system (Cyrillic, Hebrew, Arabic, Chinese, etc.); we may want to be able to say a few phrases in that language, such as for hello, good morning, my name is, and so on.

As teachers, we may think that this is a strange activity to do in the classroom with monolingual students and teachers. However, if we really value languages as a resource for all of us to use, it is a good idea to model the importance of the language heritage by engaging in our own journey into multiliteracy. As with any journey, it starts with one step at a time, or one phrase at a time!

Noa's Ark Is Resting— The Journey Is on Its Way

Teachers and parents should collaborate in serious ways in order to facilitate the development of multiliteracy. In Noa's case, whenever the communication between home and school was good, multiliteracy flourished.

Let me give you one powerful example drawn from my research. At Passover time (a Jewish holiday celebrating the exodus of Jews as slaves from Egypt), Noa's teacher asked her to make a presentation to the class about Passover. The night before the presentation, Noa asked her Mom and me to tell her the story of Passover again. This was intended to help her share the story with her fellow students. In the middle of our conversation, Noa decided to take notes, which resulted in the piece of writing shown in Figure 5–1.

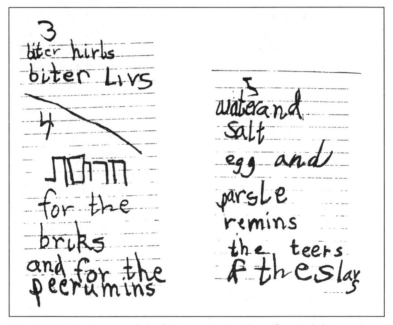

Figure 5–1. Using Cultural Assets as Catalysts for Multiliteracy Development, April 1995. *Translation: 3. Bitter herbs; bitter lives. 4. Charoses (in Hebrew) for the bricks and for the pyramids. 5. Water and salt, egg and parsley reminds the tears of the slaves.*

This is another case of positive collaboration between home and school: Both settings supported an authentic multiliteracy event in which languages were used for an authentic reason for an authentic audience. From the beginning of the year, the teacher was interested in and used Noa's knowledge about her home and cultural background as a resource for the class. Noa was proud to share her Jewish identity. She expressed her interests through writing and presentations to the class about Jewish holidays or Jewish experiences.

Remember that Noa produced only six pieces of writing in Hebrew. Because of her teacher's request, Noa researched some of the traditional foods eaten during the Passover feast. In order to do so, we used the "Seder Plate," a plate that has a Hebrew word in the different sections for different foods, which symbolize different things. During the explanation of the different foods, Noa translated most of the words into English (egg—for the destruction of the temple in Jerusalem, etc.) However, when she reached the word *charoset* (in Hebrew), she was not able to translate it. Instead, she copied the word in Hebrew from the Seder plate to her notes! (Charoset, by the way, is a mixture of apples or dates and nuts that is eaten during the Passover feast in order to remember the color of the bricks of the pyramids, which, according to the Jewish tradition, were built by the Jewish people before they fled from Egypt). This was one of the most important multiliteracy events that Noa participated in during the year, and it was inspired by Noa's teacher.

After presenting to different groups of teachers vignettes like this and the findings of my research, many have asked me, "How does your research on Noa's journey help me develop multiliteracy in my own class?" The following are some practical tools and ideas that can be developed to fully foster students' literacy, biliteracy, or multiliteracy development.

Encourage Students' Presentations and Discussions on Their Cultural Assets as Catalysts for Multiliteracy Development

Noa's teacher very wisely used Noa's background and cultural assets as a catalyst for multiliteracy development. She invited Noa to share with the class throughout the year issues related to her Jewish background. From the interviews with the teacher, it is clear that, in doing so, she was trying to promote multicultural understandings in the class. I will argue that, on the other hand, she was unaware of the impact her effort had on Noa's multiliteracy development, which followed Noa's interest in her cultural background.

When we discuss some of our home traditions, we usually code switch the foreign word into English: bar mitzvah, quinceañera, fajitas, pow-wow, and so forth. We could translate the word by explaining the meaning of the word, but it may take us longer. Therefore, most often, we include the word from our home language in our English explanation and then explain its meaning in English as best as we can.

I believe that Noa's teacher unintentionally created a wonderful multiliteracy learning opportunity for us to follow: Include students' home cultures in your curriculum presentations. When doing so, remember that some of the terms and concepts of the cultures may be expressed in the home language. Ask your students to try to write a list of those words in their home languages, followed by the English translation, to be posted for the whole class to see. This simple tool may enhance students' literacy development in their home languages.

It is clear that the teacher's interest in Noa's heritage and language has had an impact on the informant's perception of the importance of her writings for others. If, as teachers, we cherish our students' writings, they become more and more conscious of their home languages' value.

Encourage the Use of "Family Language Trees" in Your Class

You may remember that Noa studied in a regular first-grade bilingual class in Tucson. Is it possible that you may have students that use different languages in different communities and situations? Could it be that we did not ask and, therefore, we did not know? I would argue that developing a map of languages used and known in your own family/class/community may help teachers understand that multiliteracy development is possible and that there are many members of the students' communities that could help in this endeavor. A child living on a reservation in the Southwest may have a father that comes from a Navajo-speaking community and a mother from a Tohono O'odham–speaking community. Moreover, both sides of the family may use some written and spoken Spanish, because part of their family lives across the Mexican border. Or a Chinese student studying in the United States public school system may have a father that comes from a Mandarin-speaking community, while the mother may come from a Cantonese speaking community, and they both live now in the United States and use English in their everyday life.

Encourage Multilingual and Bilingual Students' Research on Language Usage

To create a multiliterate class, there is a need to create some dialogue in the class around such issues as the following:

- Language Usage: As with Noa's family, language may be used as an inclusive device, or as an exclusive device in the class. Some students may feel excluded

when a group of students may speak, read, or write in
their own languages. On the other hand, in a
multiliterate class, we need to provide opportunities
for students to use their languages and be aware of
the various implications of language usage in the
different families and communities.

- Melting Pot: It may be very important for your
minority students' parents (as well as for Noa's
parents) that children learn the language of the
country in which they live now. It is also important to
view other languages as resources. We should
encourage multiliteracy development by adding new
languages to the child's repertoire, instead of
promoting the more common situation of encouraging
English learning and forgetting about fostering our
students' mother tongues.

Encourage Monolingual Students' Research on Their Own Families' and Communities' Language Use

Many American children come from families that used different languages in prior generations. It may be useful to research our own families' language experiences. We may
start by asking our grandma if she knows any song, word,
sentence, or expression in any language other than English.
We may also ask her if there is any other member of the
family that may know how to read or write in that language,
and so on. Researching our own language background is
crucial in order to foster multiliteracy in our classrooms.

It is important to promote good communication between the home and the school. Noa's teacher invited us to
come to school to share aspects of Noa's background. However, the teacher never asked Noa to read or write in Hebrew. Although there is no need for teachers to know the
languages that their students know in order to promote their

multiliteracy development, teachers could ask parents to come to school and read for the children; they could ask older siblings to write for younger siblings; they could set aside one hour a week for reading in the different languages; they could have a collection of books, magazines, tapes, and so forth, in the different languages; they could display different alphabets in the classroom; and they could encourage their students to develop a diary in their own languages. All of these experiences would promote students' multiliteracy development. Noa's teacher, although very interested in Noa's Jewish background, did not provide Noa with challenging opportunities to develop multiliteracy.

Epilogue

Some Final Thoughts

The need for a multiliteracy agenda in education has been evident for many years. In many English as a Second Language classes, students come from different countries, using different languages in the school setting. In the school, English tends to be the only language of instruction. In bilingual settings, the teacher and the children share the two languages that are used in the school and in the home. But, as in Noa's case, sometimes children speak more than two languages. In Noa's class, there was another student, a Native American child that spoke Tohono O'odham at home. The multilingual nature of many classrooms raises interesting questions to be answered by teachers and researchers: How can I promote the languages that the children speak, and perhaps can read and write, although I am unable to speak, read, or write them? Do I need to be multilingual in order to foster a multilingual curriculum?

A teacher that knows about language development and language learning and teaching does not need to be multilingual and multiliterate in order to develop multiliteracy in the class. Using Noa's classroom as an example, in which the teacher knew English and Spanish, it is easy to conclude that her idea of a bilingual class was very limited, as she never attempted to further Noa's interest in Hebrew development. I did not find even one example in which the teacher asked Noa to bring a Hebrew book to the class for her to show or to read to the children. Her teacher showed no interest in the Hebrew alphabet, for example.

It is my opinion that teachers have many opportunities to further students' interest in their own native languages. I think that a good language teacher should ask students to bring in children's books that represent all the languages that they speak. The teacher could ask parents to come to the class to read from these books to the students. The children could start diaries in their native languages in order to further their multiliteracy development. The teacher may not be able to read the diaries or books, but, if he or she encouraged the children to share their home languages; involved the home, if appropriate; and showed interest in the results, that would further develop the students' range of experiences with their native languages.

Multiliteracy development is a challenging topic of research. However, it seems to be one of the least researched topics in teacher education programs. Noa's research has helped me realize that knowledge about how multiliteracy learning and teaching can be promoted is important for enhancing students' multiliteracy development.

Let me finish with a language story about Noa's multi-literacy. Noa was asked by her new teacher in her new school in Overland Park, Kansas, to write something about herself by completing the sentence starter, "I am special because . . . ." Noa wrote the following sentence: "I am special because I know how to read and write in many different languages."

Appendix

First Attempts at Analysis

My first approach to managing the "mountains" of data was to start a folder according to the month of the study and put together all the written pieces for that particular month. Even this very simple decision wasn't very easy to follow. What constitutes a written piece for a first grader? This differentiation in a first-grader's writing samples is quite complex. I used a simple but important differentiation parameter: If there was any written statement written by the writer as a written representation of oral language, I regarded that piece as a writing piece, even if nonlanguage symbols were evident. If the piece included only numerals, drawings, musical notations, or math problems, I did not include it in this analysis.

The second problem was to define what is a "written piece." Is a dialogue journal only one written piece, or is every entry in the dialogue journal a written piece? Is a holiday journal, written as an assignment for the winter holidays, one written piece, although it included twenty-six written pages? The best way that I found to create the limits of the written pieces was to try to understand the context and the boundaries of the meaning trying to be constructed. Noa was trying to convey several ideas throughout her journal writing; on several occasions, the teacher answered them, so I viewed the different entries as different written pieces. On the other hand, while Noa was writing her twenty-six-page winter journal, she was aware that the audience for this piece of writing was going to read it and construct the meaning from the beginning to the end of the piece. Therefore, I considered the whole winter journal as only one piece.

References

Aguirre, A. 1988. "Code-Switching, Intuitive Knowledge, and the Bilingual Classroom." In *Ethnolinguistics Issues in Education,* eds. H.S. Garcia & R.C. Chavez. Lubbock: Texas Tech University, College of Education.

Atwell, N. 1987. *In the Middle: Writing, Reading and Learning with Adolescents.* Portsmouth, NH: Boynton/Cook.

Carney, T. 1992. "Mountain or Mole Hill: The Genre Debate Viewed from Down Under." *Reading* 26 (1): 23–29.

Calkins, L.M. 1986. *The Art of Teaching Writing.* Portsmouth, NH: Heinemann.

Cummins, J. 1984. "Language Proficiency and Academic Achievement Revisited: A Response." In *Language Proficiency and Academic Achievement,* ed. C. River, 71–76. Avon, England: Multilingual Matters.

Delgado-Gaitan, C., & H. Trueba. 1991. *Crossing Cultural Borders: Education for American Families in America.* Bristol, PA: Falmer Press.

Fagan, W.T. 1995. "Literacy Learning Outside the Classroom." *The Reading Teacher* 49 (3): 260–62.

Ferreiro, E., & A. Teberosky. 1982. *Literacy Before Schooling.* Exeter, NH: Heinemann Educational Books.

Goodman, K.S. 1990. "Whole Language at the Chalk-face." In *The Whole Language Catalog,* eds. K.S. Goodman, L.B. Bird & Y.M. Goodman, 281–83. Santa Rosa, CA: American School Publishers.

Goodman, K.S. 1996. *On Reading.* Portsmouth, NH: Heinemann.

Goodman, K.S., Y.M. Goodman & B. Flores. 1979. *Reading in the Bilingual Classroom: Literacy and Biliteracy.* Rosslyn, VA: National Clearinghouse for Bilingual Education.

Goodman, Y.M. & S. Wilde. 1992. *Literacy Events in a Community of Young Writers.* New York: Teachers College Press.

Graves, D.H. 1983. *Writing: Teachers and Children at Work.* Portsmouth, NH: Heinemann.

Hall, N. 1991. "Play and Emergent Literacy." In *Play and Early Literacy Development,* ed. J.F. Christie, 3–26. Albany: State University of New York Press.

Halliday, M.A.K. 1975. *Learning How to Mean.* London: Edward Arnold.

———. 1979. "Three Aspects of Children's Language Development: Learning Language, Language as a Means Toward an End and Language as an End in Itself." In *Oral and Written Language Development Research: Impact on Schools,* eds. Y.M. Goodman, M.M. Haussler, & D.S. Strickland. Newark, DE: International Reading Association.

Harste, D., J. Woodward, & C. Burke. 1984. *Language Stories and Literacy Lessons.* Exeter, NH: Heinemann Educational Books.

Huerta, A.G. 1977. "The Acquisition of Bilingualism: A Code-Switching Approach." In *Working Papers in Sociolinguistics 39.* Austin, TX: Southwest Educational Development Laboratory.

Kelder, R. 1996. Rethinking Literacy Studies from the Past to Present. (ERIC Document 417373).

Krashen, S. 1990. *Inquiries and Insights: Second Language Teaching, Immersion and Bilingual Education Literacy, Selected Essays.*

Lanteigne, B., & D. Schwarzer. 1997. "The Progress of Rafael in English and Family Reading: A Case Study." *Journal for Adolescent and Adult Literacy* 41 (1): 36–45.

Leopold, W.F. 1939. *Speech Development of a Bilingual Child: A Linguist's Record,* vols. 1 & 2. Evanston, IL: Northwestern University Press.

Martin, J.R. 1991. "Critical Literacy: The Role of a Functional Model of Language." *Australian Journal of Reading* 14 (2): 117–32.

McLaughlin, B. 1984. "Early Bilingualism: Methodological and Theoretical Issues." In *Early Bilingualism and Child Development,* eds. M. Paradise & Y. Lebrun. Holland: Swets & Zeitilinger.

Moll, L.C. 1988. "Some Key Issues in Teaching Latino Students." *Language Arts* 65 (5): 465–72.

Moll, L.C. & S. Diaz. 1987. "Change as the Goal of Educational Research." *Anthropology in Education Quarterly* 18 (4): 300–11.

Peyton, J.K., & L. Reed. 1990. *Dialogue Journal Writing with Nonnative English Speakers: A Handbook for Teachers.* Alexandria, Va: Tesol, Inc.

Pfaff, C.W. 1979. "Constraints on Language Mixing." *Language* 55: 291–318.

Piaget, J. 1971. *Science of Education and the Psychology of the Child.* New York: Viking.

Pitcher, E.G., & E. Prelinger. 1963. *Children Tell Stories: An Analysis of Fantasy.* New York: International University Press.

Poplack, S. 1983. "Intergenerational Variation in Language Use and Structure in a Bilingual Context." In *An Ethnographic/Sociolinguistic Approach to Language Proficiency Assessment,* ed. C. Rivera. Avon, England: Multilingual Matters.

Quintero, E., & A. Huerta-Macias. 1990. "All in the Family: Bilingualism and Biliteracy. " *The Reading Teacher* 44 (4): 306–12.

Rosenblatt, L. 1978. *The Reader, the Text, the Poem.* Carbondale, IL: Southern Illinois University.

Schieffelin, B. & C. Smith. 1984. "Learning to Read Culturally: Literacy Before Schooling." In *Awakening to Literacy,* eds. H. Goelman, A. Oberg & F. Smith. Exeter, NH: Heinemann Educational Books.

Schwarzer, D., R.E. Kahn, & K. Smart. 2000. "Learning Contracts and Team Teaching in a University ESL Writing Class." *The Internet TESL Journal* 6 (10): October 2000. http://www.aitech.ac.jp/~iteslj/Articles/Schwarzer-Contracts.html

Tukinoff, W.J. 1985. *Applying Significant Bilingual Instruction Features in the Classroom.* Rosslyn, VA: National Clearinghouse of Bilingual Education.

Whitmore, K.F. & C.G. Crowell. 1994. *Inventing a Classroom: Life in a Bilingual Whole Language Learning Community.* York, ME: Stenhouse Publishers.

Wilde, S. 1992. *You Kan Red This! Spelling and Punctuation for Whole Language Classrooms, K-6.* Portsmouth, NH: Heinemann.

Wortman, R.C. 1991. "Authenticity in the Writing Events of a Whole Language Kindergarten/First Grade Classroom." Unpublished doctoral dissertation, University of Arizona, Tucson.